The True & Only Wealth of Nations: | Essays on Family, Economy & Society

The True & Only Wealth of Nations: Essays on Family, Economy & Society

Louis de Bonald

Translated by
Christopher Olaf Blum

Sapientia **Press**
of Ave Maria University

Requests for permission to make copies of any part of the work should be directed to:

Sapientia Press
of Ave Maria University
1025 Commons Circle
Naples, FL 34119
888-343-8607

Cover Image: Millais, Sir John Everett (1829–1896)
Christ in the House of His Parents. 1849–50. Oil on canvas, 86.4 × 139.7 cm.
Tate Gallery, London, Great Britain

Photo Credit : Tate Gallery, London/Art Resource, NY

Cover Design: Eloise Anagnost

Printed in the United States of America.

Library of Congress Control Number: 2006928345

ISBN-10: 1-932589-31-7

ISBN-13: 978-1-932589-31-3

| Table of Contents

Foreword: In Defense of Louis de Bonald or the Nature of Human Societies

B ONALD HAS not been a prophet in his own country: He lies under layers of dust swept over him by the relentless winds of democratic hatred and fear. He was partially exhumed some years ago, just so everyone could glimpse enough of his corpse to see what a monster of a man he was; in a few inept pages introducing excerpts of his work,[1] one is presented with a deranged preacher, fanatically obsessed with a personal hatred of individual freedom. He is an obsessive authoritarian, obviously bordering on fascism or totalitarianism, building his fantastic schemes upon the scurrilous notion that there might be a nature of man, a nature of societies, a nature of things. Better to seal his coffin once and for all.

I

Needless to say, there are times when such obviously innate cretinism puts one in awe of what nature can achieve. But then there are respites, almost miraculous ones, such as Mr. Blum's effort to reopen Bonald's case. Whatever Bonald's shortcomings, his views of man as a sociable animal make him one of the last representatives in modern times of a tradition that dates back to the beginnings of our civilization. This tradition is not only an object of curiosity: Its perennial longevity bears witness to a wisdom our contemporaries choose to ignore out of sheer arrogance and a presumptuous inability to see beyond our limited horizon. Even though his unraveling of natural processes may not be much more effective for people of our times than the description of his cells' degeneration for a patient in the terminal throes of cancer, one must assume there somewhere remains among our fellowmen some curiosity about what health used to be.

Bonald's political philosophy, though it may not be all-inclusive, nevertheless gives pretty good, if sometimes exotic, hints about where to look for true and realistic principles.

II

Ever since Plato, philosophers have been inquiring into what, in the timeless vortex of ceaseless becoming, can be considered as true or false, real or illusory, good or bad (the Greeks used to add beautiful or ugly). This is what philosophy was all about: what things really are—including human beings. One could argue that nowadays philosophy has passed away: The very idea that things have a nature has become meaningless. Contrary to popular notion, even scientists couldn't care less; they are perfectly satisfied with knowing how things generally behave (on a repetitive basis) when one interferes with them. (Honest scientists will therefore confess never to hold anything to be true, but only valid until further notice.) That sort of relativism is precisely what Bonald, as a true philosopher, tries to overcome. He believes—very rightly so, if I may say—that whatever man may scheme and attempt to build according to his own ideas is unnatural, precisely because it is an artifact (a product of his art). Every being has a nature that is but the way it is in order to keep existing as it is, that is, for animated beings to keep living. The nature of an animal is the sum total of all the components it needs to live; it is the total of the built-in features that allow it to live. Nature is the internal organization of all beings that enables them to fight and resist death (so much so that death itself is unnatural; no individual animal really dies, because it can reproduce itself, and that protective process is a tributary to nature itself). Even modern science has been unable to change the simple fact that reproduction of human life demands that it be transmitted jointly by a man and a woman, and that barring some upheaval of nature with men turning into snails, reproduction will remain thus, because that is the way things are by nature.

Now why should one assume that only physical things have a nature? Is there any reason there should not be such a thing as a nature of man considered as a spiritual and not only as a physical being? Bonald does not think there is any, and his inquiry immediately becomes an inquiry into the nature of things spiritual, moral, and social.

Let us stop here a few moments. We are at a crossroad, the one, I think, at which Bonald, and all reasonable men, definitely part company with our contemporaries. The latter are literally addicted to this creed of theirs, that man is a creature naturally enjoying a state of perfect freedom to order his actions, dispose of his possessions and persons as he thinks fit (as Locke put it in his *Second Treatise*, particularly insisting on man not having to ask leave or depending on the will of any other man).[2] We shall see Bonald is very much indeed attached to man's freedom, but it is a freedom that is in awe of nature, that is to say the type of freedom considered moot by any self-respecting man of progress: How, indeed, this man will say, can a man be free if fettered by his own nature? Since man's essence is perfect freedom, such a restriction to this freedom amounts to a claim to deprive him of his manhood, his dignity (an argument that would not have been lost on Jean-Jacques Rousseau). Men of science concur: Most contemporary scientific feats are just as many steps taken for everyone plainly to be satisfied that man's only nature is to make his nature (to be his own maker), which is just another way of saying he has no nature, since the only one he acknowledges is indeed an artificial one. But this arrogant claim is precisely what Bonald is convinced to be the most lethal for mankind; ignoring one's nature is the most foolproof way to one's death. To him this seems to be the most blatant, the sheerest common-sensical truth. But moderns are dedicated to their dream of omnipotence, and who can shake them out of their stupor? The temptation—the essence of all temptations—to fulfill any dream man may nurture was born with man himself, and it is all too easy to cast Bonald into the role of a sick old party pooper, obsessively intent on preventing everyone from enjoying life (never mind that any doctor will tell you to beware of drugs!).

By the same token it should be noted—especially by the modern mind—that the reference to nature definitely sets Bonald apart from any conceivable utopia; he is no more a dreamer, sordid or lunatic, than a physician describing a healthy organism. He is not intent on imposing any scheme, he is merely investigating the ways any society works. From his point of view, the moderns are the true utopians; they discard the past, the wisdom of an experience that reflects nature, and having built their cities in the clouds, they unfortunately try to turn them into earthly ones. While the moderns are at liberty to deny any substance to the idea of nature, by doing so, it should be pointed out, they stand to face a difficulty symmetrical to the one they are confronting Bonald with; if nothing is natural (or anything is just as natural as anything else), where is the standard for men to evaluate their thoughts and actions? But here is where Bonald lands a blow. Either there is none, and mankind faces chaos, or the only possible one is for everyone to agree on some measure of common standard (what is true or good is just what everyone agrees with the others to be true or good). But Bonald's point is precisely that given a society in which everything rests exclusively upon individual agreement, and nothing is validated merely because it is natural, this society has no stability, no peace, no enduring structure; it is a totally artificial body, which, if it works at all cannot but decay rapidly, precisely because it is artificial.

III

With this in mind, let us turn toward Bonald's definition of man's nature and what he calls the natural laws of society—any society. To him, there are principles that are like springs from which any social organism draws its life. It seems to me that according to him there are four.

The first (from which flow the three others) is an old one, but somewhat revisited. Bonald's man is undoubtedly a social animal, that is, an animal that needs society to reach the accomplishment of his own nature (a man who has not been brought up in a social environment would not talk, and what is a man incapable of speech?). Bonald's man is from the start the reverse of Rousseau's; solitude turns him into a brute or requires that he be a god. But I think there is more to Bonald's conception of man's sociability than even the old Aristotelian idea. For Bonald, man's propensity for society runs much deeper than the need to exchange goods or services to better his material life, or even ideas to improve his mind. Obviously in Bonald's eyes the reason for man's sociability lies in his likeness to God, that is to say that just as God's love is diffusive of itself in the act of creating man, it is in the nature of man, as an image of God, to go beyond himself, to transmit what he has received—that is, to "love his neighbor." The ultimate reason for man's sociability is in the last analysis a theological one.

Is that setting the bar unreasonably high? Why should it not be enough to see society as the only means for men to live less precarious lives, or develop their minds by discussion, dialogue, and reciprocal intellectual education? Bonald's answer is very clear and reflects his acute realism; the bar can never be set high enough because the only thing that matches man's natural proclivity to society is man's equally natural reluctance to society. Is man's nature contradictory? Yes, answers Bonald, it is, and it is entirely natural that it be so. As a Christian, Bonald is plainly at no odds with the idea that sin has ruined the original harmony of man's nature. But as a philosopher in search of the nature of things, he is faced with this very simple fact supported by perennial experience and always accessible to anyone: While being called society by his nature, any man is by himself a living entity also, a whole in his own right, whose primary natural concern is to survive as an individual. Rousseau was not entirely mistaken judging each man to be "a perfect and solitary whole"; that is also the nature of a living body attached to his own integrity. Henceforth sheer realism imposes the enforcement of the idea that no man can enter society before he has shed his propensity to be a world unto himself; to Bonald, participation in a society and man's natural egoism are mutually exclusive, being a social animal is being a continually self-sacrificing animal. This is precisely why man's sociability requires some help—and it would not hurt if that help were not entirely human.

IV

That is to say man must be educated, which is the second natural law of human societies.

Moderns, faced with the basic fact of individual self-love, both bow to it as if it were a sacred law of nature, and proclaim the godlike quality of the individual, then are faced with the impossible task of drawing a society out of the very unsociability of mankind; this is why they end up claiming that men are able to live together peacefully only because they pretend men are aware of the necessity to respect one another's freedom (Locke's law of nature). But, to the French Rights of Man, Bonald prefers honesty. Any unfettered freedom, and especially a freedom proclaimed to be a natural right, is bound to enter into war with another one; a backstage, hypocritical—not openly declared—war, maybe, which will be called society, but a war all the same, in which the battle cries are protestations of friendship and cooperation. So much so that Bonald, running afoul of contemporary irenic pacifism, chooses to frankly state the necessity to curb the individual's natural lawlessness, to tame the wild animal in him. There can be no society, thinks Bonald, unless some kind of devotion to others overcomes the individual's adoration of himself.

A good citizen is the man who serves his country, not a man who makes good business out of his fellowmen. Our times extol the individual and marvel at the growing crime rate; they embody the age of "Endarkenment's" dogma (to borrow Thomas Fleming's felicitous wording) and go about parroting Jean-Jacques Rousseau: Man is naturally good, something must have corrupted him, most probably evil men (hence scaffolds, always more scaffolds). Bonald's idea is that even though a sociable individual is in itself an oxymoron (any individual is born an egoistic and rather wild creature), nevertheless man carries within himself a good heart and a minimum of understanding; but it is in the shape of a potential that, like his ability to speak, has to be nurtured, cared for, developed. In other words, in Bonald's world no scaffolds are needed, but rather schools and teachers; no man is born perfect, he has to be educated. Society among men demands they be brought up morally and spiritually first and foremost.

But is not mandatory education what all good democrats have been after ever since the French Revolution? Hardly. The education of a man is not the taming of a wild beast; it aims not at building reflexes meaningless to the animal (*"Donnez-moi de bonnes lois, je vous donnerai de bons citoyens,"* St. Just used to say), but at drawing out of a man what is inside him. Nobody ever learns anything natural that is not what he already knows. Self-education, however, is at best a rare ability, because it meets resistance (it is always more fun to play than to study), especially when it demands the individual himself overcome his own natural self-centered nature. It is one thing to learn about the faces of the moon—that is, for education to address the intellect, but it is an altogether different thing for anybody to fight his own nature—that is, for education to ensure that the benevolent impulses of the human heart prevail over the natural selfishness of one's intellect. In other words if educating a man means inculcating him with the habit of devoting himself to others rather than exclusively to himself, it takes some outside help to achieve its purpose. There is no teaching without a teacher having some authority and power over his pupils.

To achieve its purpose nature therefore requires that power not be disseminated into too many hands, but rather concentrated in as few as possible, and ideally those of only one man. It is an old argument that dates back at least to St. Thomas. If a society is to be a unified body of men, it needs a visible symbol of its unity as well as a unifying power that cannot act more efficiently as such than when it belongs to one man. But Bonald's case is even more specific. The main evil threatening society lies for him in that invention of modern times, the unfettered, self-righteous, self-centered, and ever-demanding individual bent on being a selfish whole within the whole and therefore destructive of any social bond. If society means anything, it means some kind of brotherhood, friendship, and, to borrow Aristotle's topic word, some *sunpneuma* (propensity to breathe together); a society is a moral being. Bonald certainly hates despotism and loves freedom,[3] but he is no liberal. For him no society results from the balance of conflicting particular interests, whether they be those of the individual, economic lobbies, social classes, or political parties. As La Fontaine would have said, the social body is made of parts inasmuch as it has organs, not of parts that each fight for leadership. In this respect Bonald sides with Rousseau, whom he dislikes, against Montesquieu, whom he admires (and whom, one should add, he has probably not understood very well). Divisive egoism is the enemy of society—the essence of which is devotion to a common purpose—as well as the enemy of mankind itself ("My name is legion" said Satan). This means that nature requires that there be a *res publica*, an interest that is not the sum of particular interests but supersedes all particular empirical ones, while being at the same time the very own interest of each citizen (the common good of classical thinking)—and while good citizens may respect the common good, which is theirs though they are still private citizens, nature also teaches that public interest is never to be so visible and tangible to all as when it belongs to a man whose nature is not to be private but public, a man who by nature cannot have any personal interest other than the general one, an essentially disinterested man. So nature finally teaches that such a man cannot be but unique (and here nature is simply logical: If there is to be unity in a whole, there cannot be several identical expressions of that unity).

Now, if society means an educated citizenry, who can be the educators?

V

There are three main candidates.

The first candidate, but not the leading one, is the family, on two counts.

First the individual is not only a destructor of society, he is also a sort of fake substance; no man is an island, all men are born and raised in families, which is the original natural society that corresponds to the social nature of man. The family, not the individual, is therefore the basic brick of the social building, and anything that endangers the family, like divorce, also endangers the whole society. Bonald has not forgotten Aristotle. Second, within the family lies the first model of the authority necessary to unite the social body; the benevolent altruistic authority of the father, which, though not devoid of coercive power, is inspired by the love of his offspring, the paternal authority aiming at nothing but to serve.[4] No doubt that in Bonald's mind this conception has some theological background (God is the father of all men), but it does not lack empirical evidence either. That said, Bonald, again after Aristotle, is far from viewing the family as the last word of man's sociability. On the contrary, the family is no more for him than the first knot of the woven social fabric; notwithstanding their inherent weakness due to their small sizes, Bonald argues with surprising realism and probably the experience of the loving father he was, that there is such a thing as a family selfishness. For a social body to exist, some superior authority is therefore needed to bond families together. Families are fundamental elements of society, but they are only elements with which society must still be built, and in the last analysis, by one single authority.

That superior authority is two-sided.

Authority means a combination of raw power and legitimacy; authority is power, but power used exclusively for the benefit of those who obey it, power motivated by the love and care for those subjected to it. Bonald is undoubtedly no anarchist, but no one has equated power and service more adamantly; even sheer property is laden with duties to others. Bonald would also say: "Do not ask yourself what your country can do for you, but what you can do for your country." If society requires moral education, it requires some Cincinnatus who accepts power but has no longing for it.

As an authority it is more than raw power: It is a power that is somehow willingly obeyed; it draws its effectiveness from the very will and mind of the citizens subjected to it. In other words it is first and foremost a power that addresses the souls, it is a spiritual power that does not force but tries to attract and convert. And to convert to what, if not to society itself? Or rather to convert to the truth of the very principle of any society, which has never varied because it is the only natural or logical one—that is to say, the love of one's neighbor, the willingness to help, the satisfaction of taking part in something that goes beyond oneself, the joy of serving. This message cannot be human, neither in its origin (why, except for purely subjective reasons, love one's neighbor, which confines love to a very restricted circle?) nor in its content (a man may have followers, he may preach the love of one's neighbors, but then his followers will do as he says, not out of love for their neighbors but out of love for him; only God can teach that one must love one's neighbors). Henceforth reason and observation, according to Bonald, clearly show who can wield the spiritual power, and who has always done it for two millenia: And who if not the Church? Not only, claims Bonald, any society demands a power that can unite the hearts (a religious one, religion coming from *religare*), but the western world has had the luck to inherit directly the Good News, ever since relayed by the Catholic Church, which is no god, but bears God's word. Is it necessary to add that by nature there cannot be two or more churches competing for the job?

But Bonald has amply shown that any individual can resist his own heart *(video meliora deteriora sequor)*. Any authority has a less ethereal side, any school master must be able to enforce attention from his pupils; there is a physical side to moral authority that it should not disregard lest it be too easily ridiculed.[5] But this power does not belong to its trustee to use as he pleases. This power aims to serve, which means its goals are set; the trustee's actions are regulated, his might both supreme and subordinate, his glory selfless dedication to the common weal. Power for Bonald is never enjoyable and something to long for: It is a duty, an office, and therefore a trust.

This type of power exists at two levels. On one hand Bonald is no democrat if only because there are fewer citizens who would rather manage a public office than their private interests, and many more who would rather use the former as a means to the latter. A natural society does not call on all of its citizens to prefer serving the others rather than themselves, nor does it make any room for the familiar figure of the politician attached to politics as a quick way to make a fortune. But there is a lot to be said for the great numbers of men who are capable of selflessness and who, like career officers, are genuinely attached to a life of service.

Let's say there are noble men, normal men, and ignoble men. Even noble men could not hold to their dedication if they were not simple auxiliaries of the power that is vested in the king. Of course Bonald makes no mystery of his being a monarchist, but the real catch is why he thinks only a king can meet the needs of a society. We already know that the unity of all parts is best warranted by the unity of will that is supposed to regulate their diversity. But I think Bonald has another reason in mind that is both rather intricate and quite inspiring. I have no doubt that the circumstances of Louis XVI's death played a decisive part in Bonald's meditation. A man may be transformed by his own role, but there are roles that somehow force the individual to transcend his own capacities and endow him with a higher stature than his spontaneous one—and such is a king's. It is not unreasonable to think that the demands of such a function may draw the individual out of himself, and that eventually he cannot think of himself as a private person any more. All in all a rather mediocre private person, namely the hapless Louis XVI, ended up acting as if he belonged so little to himself that it was only natural for him to give his own life for the redemption of his kingdom. Dying almost as a martyr, he actually bore witness to what a king can ultimately be, a man emulating Christ. In other words, a king in Bonald's mind, while certainly not a god, is not exactly a man any more; he is only the visible shape taken by something that is beyond him and that prevents his power from being something Bonald could not condone any more than Jean-Jacques Rousseau could, the power of a man upon a man. That many kings were obviously far from this ideal standard does not prevent it from standing as a measure of their worth as kings. And who ever said that an unworthy king does not eventually meet the fate he deserves? Be that as it may, it is the moral nature of the royal function that makes it for Bonald such a plausible and realistic figure of political power: A king need not be a genius, nor even extremely clever, he only has to be as virtuous and exemplary a man as possible. And Bonald, true to Aristotelian teaching, knew that virtue has a lot more to do with habit than with understanding; that therefore if it cannot be taught, properly speaking, at least it can be inculcated by proper education, especially if reinforced by longstanding family tradition. This is yet another reason for Bonald's monarchist leanings.

This leads us to Bonald's third natural law of human societies.

VI

Supposing society to be organized according to nature, there remains to be seen how it can last. In the ever-changing flow of human affairs, from where can a social body possibly derive some stability and resiliency against the usual decay of everything human?

French politicians have lately taken a childish liking to primitive slogans, among which they have a favorite: to vote for me is to vote for Change (with a capital C). Change is a program, Change is an end in itself. Not so for Bonald: No one in his right mind can possibly wish to change something that is natural; a healthy society needs only to be conserved in order to remain healthy. As Bonald ceaselessly emphasizes, in any society health means virtue, that is, being devoted to others, to the public good, therefore being disinterested and infused with the spirit of service. The more citizens will consider themselves as officers, the more a society will be and remain a sane society.

Hence come Bonald's two recipes for social health, both stemming from respect for the workings of Time. (Rome was not built in a day.)

The first is the constant moral training of the citizens, the building of habitual respect for moral values, what Montesquieu called *"les moeurs."* What was true for the king is true for any citizen. Virtue is a habit, and though not everyone can be taught to be intelligent, probably anyone can be given habits. Particularly when they tend to reinforce some inner nature, some innate propensity, which has to be the case with morals. (Let us remember if this not be the case, there is no more hope for a man to enter a real society than for a wild beast forced to perform by its master's whip.) There is a catch of course: that there be enough virtuous individuals, with enough power of persuasion to maintain moral customs. Bonald thought it was an easy requirement in nineteenth-century Europe. I cannot claim it is such an easy one these days.

Even supposing it were, society must still be protected from decay over successive generations. But, Bonald seems to say, there is an obvious remedy against senescence, and again it is a natural one, built into the genes of human beings. Each man has it in himself to be almost immortal, for families are but everlasting individuals. Families are the channel through which habits can be transmitted and turned into the personal traditions to which the heirs become linked by honor and duty. True societies last because they do not need individuals eager to show off their abilities so much as long lines of sons picking up the job after their fathers' demise, with a sense of fulfilling an office. To do this they do not need talent so much as virtue. If virtue is a habit then obviously time can consolidate virtue, not only through individuals but mainly through families whose life span is indefinite. Once there are enough families endowed with respect for their own traditions, a society is really founded and built to perpetuate itself. Thus nature wants societies to hold together by a double bond: a spirit of public service on one hand, hereditary functions on the other.

Before modern protests stifle Bonald's voice, it must be observed that even though our times exert themselves going against nature, nature's natural calling is only superficially denied: Not only is it common practice among professional people, but—who has not heard of movie actors trying to pass on their trade to their sons? There are countries, such as France, where professions like the military are still a family tradition. And who can argue that good wine deteriorates with age, or know-how with antiquity of practice and experience?

All in all, this is the gist of Bonald's intuition: Nothing natural pops up in an instant, and, as everything that lasts is natural, everything that is natural takes time to grow. Our present enlightened intelligentsia notwithstanding, there is no way to frame a constitution out of the blue. So what must be opposed is not change but continuous and, above all, violent and drastic change, or ceaseless turbulence and agitation. There is no question that human affairs are in a state of imperfection that continuously asks for improvement—but reasoned, considered, and timely improvement. Thus Bonald takes great pains to stress the necessity of continuously feeding new blood into the current organism. Society needs not only virtues, it needs talents, intelligence, gifts; it should use them as much as possible but, since they come and go, without entrusting them with any function that can only be fulfilled by people of age-old experience. What else could indeed be expected from a defender of that perennial society of ever-changing members that is called the church? We are thus presented with a classic case of Bonald's common sense. What is essential to society is the ordinary fulfilling of the day-to-day satisfaction of its basic needs, which requires a diversity of professions. These professions tend by nature to be in the hands of those whose main quality is virtue, and these tend by nature to be the inheritors of a long-lasting legacy of serving. But by nature some offices that require exceptional talent should be granted to anyone displaying it (it is one of the king's duties to surround himself with virtuous men, with the counsel of clever and ambitious individuals). So all in all, every office should be open to anyone having shown himself to be of service to the community, with the assumption that some offices may become hereditary as time passes and successive generations keep display-ing the same spirit of service (those who had shed blood for their country for a significant period of time might eventually be rewarded with titles of landed property). By the same token, there may be families that degener-ate, forfeit their legacy, lose credit, and prove themselves unworthy of their status. Bonald has no doubt they will disappear naturally from the public realm. This is no rigid society, no caste system; it is orderly, non-frenetic social mobility. Bonald could say with Burke: "A disposition to preserve and an ability to improve taken together would be my standard of a states-man." Bonald is not after an immutable society; he is after a society to which every citizen may belong, that is, find the spot where he can be most useful. Thus this would be neither a democratic society, in which resentment is constantly bred by the illusory expectation that everybody is fit for everything, nor a socialist or despotic one, in which individuals are but cogs to the overwhelming whole. Plainly it is the naturally organized society that classical philosophy has advocated for centuries.

VII

Now we can understand Bonald's fourth natural law of human societies.

Despite the stupid innuendoes of his few contemporary readers, Bonald is not an authoritarian personality and does not even come close to advocating any so-called absolute monarchy. He is a man devoted to individual freedom and responsibility—but to be a free citizen in his mind is not the opposite of having a duty to perform, no more than having a responsibility is contrary to being responsible to someone.

There are some social institutions that are naturally conducive to freedom, and they appear in the forefront of Bonald's society.

One is the institution of private property. Families being the bricks natural society is built with, it is only natural that property become the mortar that both binds them together and also holds each of them together. Bonald's idea is, as usual, as simple as it is common sense: By nature there is no family where there is no family home, or more generally *"propriété de famille."* One reason is that if families are to have some substance, that is, to be some real entity, they should have some means to support themselves as such. A whole that depends on something outside it to exist is not a whole. Bonald's idea is as old as nature; any real being is somehow self-contained and self-sufficient, its own autarchy the visible proof of its particular potential perfection. But there is another reason for families to have to maintain property. The long possession of an estate, large or small, is the visible symbol of its continuity, that is to say, of its subsistence through time, and therefore of its very historical reality. Everyone has a family that dates back millennia; everyone goes back to Adam. But no family is as traceable, as obviously an entity by itself, as the family whose ancestors already owned the same building centuries ago.[6] Is it necessary to note how all that points to landed property as the type of property most befitting its natural purpose? Bonald's natural society is made up of landed families—which was still the common idea behind those famous races that took place during the American conquest of the west in which everyone could compete for a piece of uninhabited land. And it should be mentioned Bonald wished such ownership to be shared by the greatest possible number of citizens.

But if that is the case, who can accuse Bonald of any yearning for despotism? Locke was right after all: Is there a better foundation for individual freedom than material independence, which means some kind of self-sufficiency, in other words some land you can live off? Where there is no property, there is no freedom. This is so obvious that it needs no further comment.[7]

Most families, as we have seen, tend primarily to their own, and service to others is mostly restricted to their relatives or their clientele. But there are more exalted families of special interest to Bonald, families whose patrimony includes, as a sort of special calling, public service, a devotion to the community as such, and whose inheritance is the duty to serve. The same freedom enjoyed by rank-and-file families is also theirs by nature, and just as legally warranted as a private property, but even more emphatically. Here again Bonald's voice is nature's own. Is it not obvious that anyone who wants to be fair must first be immune to external pressure, which means first of all immune to the fear of losing his position? Bonald was so convinced of this truth, and so remote from any longing for absolutism, that he thought any public officer should be protected by irrevocability. We are so used to the ways of our politicians that it is difficult not to take Bonald's attitude as naive, and out of touch with reality. But this only shows how deep we have sunk, and how far from the light of nature, for what should be more natural than for a man who has chosen to enter the service of others to be a disinterested man, a virtuous one? As a matter of fact, Bonald is not so naive. His public officers do not come out of some miraculous blue, and nature points at what happens. Virtue is a habit, and chances are that disinterestedness, loyalty, and faithfulness will come all the more naturally to the man for whom those virtues represent a family tradition, an inheritance he strives to respect and feels bound to honor as part of himself. This does not mean there cannot be any new man; all blood has to be rejuvenated. But any transfusion should be checked by the wisdom of tradition; all talents should be used, but nature forbids that they overwhelm old and steady virtue. Again Bonald has nothing against freedom; he simply does not want rashness to be mistaken for it.

It should also be remembered there is no better way to ensure that a man performs his job well than to have him perform it of his own accord and trust him to do it as he thinks best; efficiency calls for freedom, slavery leads to slovenliness (which is the very opposite of the modern conception that virtue should be contrived and a man is mostly virtuous when he is in a position to be rewarded for it). To those who will object that heredity means indifference to performance, it should be pointed out that it also means responsibility toward future generations as well as toward past ones. Where there is responsibility, there must be a responsible use of freedom.

One could almost claim that Bonald's society is one in which coercion is least necessary, because where things go according to their nature, they go by themselves.

VIII

Let us conclude by conjuring up some of the most evil spirits threatening Bonald's organized city (a sort of fifth law of nature: to fight the seduction of what nature forbids). Taken together, they account for the main features of contemporary western society. Bonald must not have been seeking immediate and undisputed popularity.

The first one (which may be only the first facet of the same basic evil) is obviously the excessive development of economic activity. Far from being the backbone of true society, it is a sure recipe for its doom. Amidst an unprecedented show of easy living, we are slouching toward pauperism and the total unraveling of the social bond. Bonald joins forces with those who predict a quickening pace of crises for capitalism (resulting in particular from overproduction). He may seem to have overreacted to the nasty social effects of industrialization, urbanization, and liberal laissez-faire, but there is more insight to his critique than is the case with the standard more or less Marxist one. Even though one must collect bits and pieces to build a cohesive argument, it seems to me—unless I burden him with my own prejudices—Bonald goes way beyond opposing one political economy to another, praising one and blaming the other. His more or less explicit feeling is that it is the economy itself that is lethal to society when considered as its main dimension or goal (there is a natural economy, the principles of which appear in the excerpts following this preface). To put a vast and difficult idea in a nutshell, one could say that beyond a certain level of material well-being, there is a contradiction between the economic spirit and the public spirit or spirit of community. The latter is pregnant with the capacity to give precedence to public interest over private, whereas the former stems basically from a propensity to consider everything and everyone else as means to be used for the satisfaction of private individual interests. That is revealed particularly in the activity of commerce (the real driving force behind the mass production of material goods), because in an exchange both parties look primarily at what each can get for itself, and logically try to get as much as possible while giving as little as possible. In other words economy is the only type of social relationship that is left to individuals who have become incapable of entertaining any properly social relationship at all, and it is more an antagonistic than a friendly relationship. That this intuition is illusory or false remains entirely to be seen.[8]

The second demon endangering human sociability is democracy, and I would say roughly for the same reason. Bonald's case against this regime is considerably documented, but all his evidence illustrates one central massive accusation: Democracy is in itself disruptive of society, for the very simple reason that it rests, as on its main foundation, exposed for everyone to see, on the avowed assumption that man is not a naturally social animal, and society is an artificial body. Democracy is therefore a pure oxymoron for which modern philosophers endlessly try and fail to find any viable application. That it is so does not take long to ascertain. The basic tenet of democracy is that no man has by himself any natural right to command any other; men are all born free and therefore equal. This is absolutely true. But then once men have realized there is no society without government, instead of looking beyond anything human to find its principle of legitimacy, they are adamant that it must lie with men. But how could any man have in himself anything on which to base any power of his over his fellowman? Moderns therefore end up with the requirement that power be distributed evenly among themselves so that no one should have to bow to anyone else, and therefore can remain his own master. Since this requirement is impossible to meet, they resort to arrangements that are out of necessity spurious and can never successfully hide the bare tyranny of man over man, the total absence of public spirit, the prevalence of private interests and passions over anything else, the corruption and the waste of public money when entrusted to people for whom there is no such thing as commonweal, and in one word the sham that is freedom, equality, and fraternity in such a regime. Any man playing God ends up being but a man.

This reveals that all the demons assailing society are children of the same father: Atheism. If there is no God, every man is left to his own personal beliefs, which naturally end up in a belief in himself alone, which is to say his own interests. Where there is no God, by nature there is war, war between self-proclaimed gods. Where there is no God, there are no common moral principles, no conscience, and men are but lawless animals. Where there is no inner restraint, there must be constraint. Of course, here is the rub: Even if one agrees to the necessity of God, how can there be one, and the same time beings endowed with the freedom to ignore him or disfigure him? Force is of course no answer; belief is not enslavement, but voluntary submission. Reason is somehow more appropriate, but reasoning also leads to selfish calculation. So what remains is faith, and primarily faith in the ability of man to acknowledge truth, that is, his own nature. Searching for faith is the ordeal mankind has been facing ever since man started using his freedom.

IX

For Bonald the truth about the future lies in the past.

Bonald goes against the grain of the wood modern heads are made of. What can they make of him?

He will shock most of them, enough for them to stop reading and throw the book away. But, because nature cannot but prevail upon human foolishness, there will be some who will start scratching their wooden heads. Not a negligible gesture. And chances are, I think, that those doing the scratching will not belong to the official intelligentsia, the world of today's princes. A very promising expectation: Any good harvest starts with a few humble seeds. |•

—Claude Polin
Professor of Political and Social Philosophy
University of Paris–Sorbonne

NOTES

[1] L.-A. de Bonald, *Théorie du Pouvoir politique et religieux, Choix de Textes et Présentation,* ed. Colette Capitan, Edition 10–18 (Paris: Union Générale d'Éditions, 1965).

[2] Locke has trouble with the idea that man is not a sociable animal at all, and he acknowledges the possibility of a natural society among men. But his apparent concession that man has to stay "within the bounds of the law of nature" only means that man unfortunately hasn't conformed to certain laws if he intends to live in society, a conviction born out of reason, says Locke himself, and not out of "natural impulse."

[3] Cf. paragraph 6.

[4] The feminists will undoubtedly jump out of their trousers at such a display of male chauvinism. I refer them to Bonald's writings; he does not even think of turning women into slaves, he insists on the mother's authority as well as the father's. But where strength is required, Bonald, being simple-minded, thinks it lies naturally with the father rather than the mother.

[5] Of course this is exactly what moderns are so quick to point out, and the more clever Catholics should agree: The church's power is not power of physical coercion, but it should have some power. Contradiction? No. There is a delicate but very real middle way between despotism and total license. But it takes men honestly looking for truth to use it. It could also be asked: Why bother with a king? Would not a pope be enough? The answer, I think, is simple. Theocracy deprives men of any responsibility or freedom, it turns men into puppets of God, and eventually puppets in the hands of tyranny claiming to be God in mortal guise.

[6] This ownership potentially entails some kind of independence of the family with regard to the State, another proof that Bonald is no enemy of personal freedom. It also warrants the identification of children with their family; whose children would they be if they owed their very existence to someone else? This is precisely why the French revolutionaries attempted to break up families as an obstacle to the absolute power of the State they were trying to set up. They proposed all children should be raised together at the State's expense.

[7] Except one: whereas Locke's property is essentially individualistic, as can be expected, for Bonald it is an essentially communal thing; even if it is headed

by the *pater familias*, it does not properly belong to him, rather he belongs to it. Any property indeed involves a double duty; any property is an office in its own right. Property does not entitle the owner to use and abuse. Bonald echoes the Christian tradition against the Roman law; property benefits the owners, familiars, or more loosely those around them in need of help, and not the owner alone, and then it must be kept up and transmitted for the use of future generations as a trust only momentarily in the hands of its manager.

8 Let us point out that Bonald is by no means indifferent to the well-being of his fellowman, impervious to any economic consideration. On the contrary he obviously sides with all those who denounce the infamies of developing capitalism. But he should not, I think—so his views on economy show clearly—be ranked among the first promoters of what is usually called the social doctrine of the Church. Right from the start, *Rerum novarum* limited the span of its critique of the modern world. It was not to be, in the wake of Pius IX's *Quanta Cura and Syllabus*, a radical one, but rather an attempt to reunite Catholic faith and capitalism; it was to be a plea for sharing, for redistribution of wealth. Bonald goes much deeper, and strikes gold: The real problem with the modern world is that it is modern, that it rejects nature. There is a natural economy (the principle of which has been referred to) and there is the modern economy, which is destructive of every social bond, because it is destructive of its primary agent, that is, a reverence for immaterial interests. Since Leo XIII, no pope ever dared come close to Bonald's and Pius IX's truth.

| A Note on the Texts

WITH THE exception of the selection from *Primitive Legislation*, to which the title "The Family in Society" has been given, all of the texts appear under close approximations of their original titles, and other than the excerpts from his speeches before the Chamber of Deputies, in their original form, with two exceptions. I have taken the liberty of dropping a three-page quotation from an obscure Napoleonic document that was made by Bonald at the close of his remarks about the civil registries; the passage was tiresome and added nothing to his argument. I have also lightly edited his 1829 essay "On Pauperism," which contained several direct quotations from his earlier essay "On the Wealth of Nations" that, in the present context, seemed best not to repeat. In several instances, I have unburdened his texts of a number of his original footnotes when it seemed to me that they were not essential to his argument. Where possible, I have incorporated material from footnotes into the text. The footnotes to the present text are mine. Bonald's remaining notes have been placed at the end of each entry. Finally, Bonald italicized words that he took to have an important technical significance. I have followed his practice only where I thought the italicization added a crucial nuance to the argument.

The texts for the translations have been taken from the Brussels edition of the *Oeuvres de Monsieur de Bonald*, published in eight volumes in 1845 by the Société Nationale pour la propagation des bons livres (The National Society for the Propagation of Good Books), with the lone exception of "On Political Economy," which did not appear in that edition and was taken directly from *Le Défenseur* of September 1820. All of the texts may also be found in the three-volume *Oeuvres complètes de M. de Bonald,* published by J.-P. Migne (Paris, 1864). |•

| Introduction

"MORALS AND laws are the true, and even the only wealth of societies, families, and nations."[1] From the heights of this lofty principle Louis de Bonald surveyed European social and political developments in the age of the French and Industrial revolutions. It was indeed a sentinel's tower from which he was able to perceive many of the grave threats to human happiness posed by the new order of things. From the inhumane conditions of factory work to the alienation of city life, from the destruction of the family to the squandering of France's forest preserves, from the decay of good morals and common decency to the first stages of the incipient welfare state: Bonald sounded the hue and cry against all these evils, and warned the wayward leaders of his time that they were presiding over the destruction of civilization. The essays and speeches gathered in this volume testify to his vigilance, as well as to the fundamental clarity of his moral vision. Time and again he condemned France and Europe for having failed to live up to the high standards of Christian civilization. The cultural crisis that was the birth of the modern world he understood to be nothing less than the repudiation of the primacy of virtue. European man had forgotten his high destiny as a creature of God and had rejected the things of the spirit in order to choose, in the name of liberty, the things of the earth. The social order could not endure such a revolution, for, as Bonald tirelessly proclaimed, society was founded upon the acknowledgment of God's existence and upon his law. Bonald's message was an admonition to an erring generation, and it was a fruitful one, to be taken up again and again in the succeeding decades as one of the principal sources feeding the great stream of criticism and commentary that led to the social encyclicals of Leo XIII and his successors.

Louis de Bonald (1754–1840), in the words of his son, Henri, was "essentially a man of the former society," that is, of the old, pre-revolutionary France.[2] He is best known, with Joseph de Maistre and Edmund Burke, as one of the first voices to have protested against the spoliation of the old Europe by the godless Revolution. Unlike Burke's *Reflections on the Revolution in France* (1790) or Maistre's *Considerations on France* (1797), Bonald's initial counter-revolutionary tract, *The Theory of Political and Religious Power* (1796), was not a rhetorical masterpiece. It was, however, the beginning of a most productive career as a Catholic publicist, a career marked especially by the patient exposition of the principles that had undergirded Europe's pre-revolutionary, Christian civilization. From *On Divorce* (1801) and *Primitive Legislation* (1802) to his *Philosophical Demonstration of the Constitutive Principle of Society* (1830), he taught the primacy of man's debts and duties to God. His genius was to have seen in detail what this principle had meant for the development of society through the many centuries of Christian civilization. As the various writings here collected demonstrate, the perceptiveness of Bonald's vision was remarkable. He saw clearly because he lived according to the truths he proclaimed.

Bonald was the only son of a landowning family from south-central France. The family seat was the chateau of Le Monna, a modest hillside estate overlooking the Dourbie river just east of Millau, a market town in the Rouergue. His father died when he was four, and he was raised by his mother; he was tutored until the age of eleven, when he was sent to Paris to continue his studies. His mother, like many in the French provincial nobility of the eighteenth century, leaned toward the stern piety of the Jansenist school, and placed her son in the charge of the Oratorians, who were known for their rigor. Bonald studied with the fathers of the Oratory at Juilly, a boarding school outside Paris, from 1769 to 1772, and his mind was marked by their Augustinian vision. All of his adult writings testify to his admiration for the great bishop Jacques-Bénigne Bossuet (1627–1704), who, while neither an Oratorian nor a Jansensist, may be counted as an Augustinian and summed up all of the austere piety and earnest conviction of the French Catholic tradition. At its best, pre-revolutionary Catholic France produced not only great saints, but sound Christian men, formed by the *Imitation of Christ* and the *Introduction to the*

Devout Life, by a code of gentlemanly honor and a spirit of Christian service. Bonald was one such man, almost the last of the breed, and he chose his motto as a sign of his creed, *Prodesse, non praeesse*, which may be rendered *to serve, not to be served*.[3]

After a tour with the royal musketeers, Bonald returned to Millau to manage his estate and to marry. He and his wife of forty-eight years, Elisabeth-Marguerite de Guibal de Combescure, had seven children, four of whom survived to adulthood. A faithful and dutiful husband, a devoted father, and, in his later years, an energetic and solicitous grandfather, Bonald was able passionately to defend the Christian family because he first loved his own family. He also loved his family's land, and these two loves were, with his love for Christ, the beacons in his life and the source of his moral vision.

Prior to the Revolution, Bonald served as mayor of Millau, a difficult task in this ancient stronghold of the Huguenots, then still suffering from religious division. Later in life he liked to recall as one of his three most cherished achievements the prevention of a riot between the Protestants and Catholics of Millau during the early days of the Revolution, when confessional strife was bloodying the streets in Nîmes, a short journey east over the rugged Cévennes uplands that were France's Calvinist heartland. In the summer of 1790, Bonald was elected to the legislative assembly for the *département* of Aveyron, where he attempted to curb the nascent egalitarianism of the Revolution. When the oath to uphold the Civil Constitution of the Clergy was promulgated in January 1791, he resigned his seat in the assembly, citing his duty to uphold the true religion. Over the course of that year, the Revolution turned markedly violent. After the king's unsuccessful attempt to flee the country in June, members of the nobility were often accused of anti-patriotic activity. In October 1791, Bonald left France, taking his two eldest sons with him to Germany. He was, apparently, just in time, for his friends in Millau soon after fell victim to the Revolution's hatred of the nobility. Bonald's wife and younger children, left behind as were the majority of émigré families, were reduced first to hiding out in a cave on their estate and then to fleeing to a family property in the east.

Bonald spent the next decade in exile from his home, first in Germany, and then, from 1797 until Napoleon's general amnesty for émigrés in

1802, in Paris. It was during this decade that the provincial public servant became a leading conservative publicist. His *Theory of Political and Religious Power* of 1796 produced little effect in France, for it was seized by the Directory and burned as seditious, but from then onward his pen was rarely idle. He first gained public notice with *Primitive Legislation*, which was reviewed favorably by Chateaubriand. *Primitive Legislation* was a systematic statement of the principles of his political philosophy. As the selection on family reproduced here attests, his theoretical project was essentially one of understanding and defending the institutions of pre-revolutionary France. Bonald was not an uncritical admirer of the old regime. He was, rather, attempting to discover and revivify the principles that had animated Christian civilization at its best. His discussion of the role of the family within a hierarchical society is notable as a sustained reflection upon a society based not upon individual autonomy but upon inherited social roles. Also of enduring value is his explanation of the educative function of the trade guilds within the broader society.

During the years of Napoleon's rule, the undisguised discussion of political topics was generally dangerous, and much of Bonald's writing accordingly took the form of literary essays and book reviews, including his 1810 notice of the French edition of Adam Smith's *Wealth of Nations*. This essay, together with his treatise on usury from 1806, show Bonald to be one of the early critics of the laissez-faire philosophy. Bonald was, in effect, the heir to the protests of the judges of the Paris Parlement against the policies of Anne-Robert-Jacques Turgot, Louis XVI's finance minister from 1774–1776. Turgot, a member of the Physiocratic school of economic liberalism, had obtained the liberalization of the grain trade and the suppression of the trade guilds, and had sought much more in the way of dismantling the regional and local privileges of French society. For Turgot and Smith, just as for Locke before them and the men of the French Revolution after them, the power of money and individual initiative was at all costs to be set free in order to effect the transformation of society. To Bonald, Turgot was the "fanatical partisan of a materialistic politics" that represented nothing less than the abandonment of the inherited understanding of justice.[4] "Wheat," Bonald wrote in another criticism of policies made famous by Turgot, "was not given to man to be an object of commerce, but to nourish him."[5] Bonald was a moralist of the old school, with a moral vision shaped by Tacitus's condemnations of Roman decadence, and he was convinced that the prescriptions of Turgot and Smith threatened nothing less than to change the very character of European man. The generous, idealistic, and chivalrous ideal of Christian civilization was, he feared, being replaced by a shrunken, narrow, and selfish vision of man.

After the restoration of Louis XVIII in 1814, Bonald was able to speak his mind more freely on political and social affairs. In the elections of the summer of 1815 to the first parliament of the Bourbon Restoration, he was chosen by his fellow Rouergats as a member of the Chamber of Deputies. The body elected in 1815 was known as the *chambre introuvable*, the chamber whose like could not be found, so conservative was its majority. To Bonald, the duty before the deputies was plain: to assist the king in undoing the Revolution's work of destruction. As it turned out, the Chamber of 1815 was able to accomplish little, for the king was hemmed in by the old Napoleonic elite, which was decidedly liberal, even anti-clerical, in its political orientation. The Chamber's one success, the repeal of legal divorce, belonged essentially to Bonald. He was known as the champion of the indissolubility of marriage thanks to his *On Divorce*,[6] and he was, therefore, granted the privilege of introducing the legislation that restored Christian marriage to France. That speech is included here, as is one written but not delivered on the need to restore to the clergy the custody of the civil registers in order to complete the restitution of marriage within French society. Both speeches contain eloquent pleas for the protection of women and children from the suffering and oppression caused by legal divorce. In addition to championing the family, Bonald sought to roll back the centralization and bureaucratization of the French government, defending, by contrast, the role of the Church and of local communities. Also included here are excerpts from his parliamentary speeches on topics ranging from the rural communes to church lands and the royal forests. It is especially in these selections that one may see the truth of Robert Nisbet's judgment that "with regard to society, group, individual, and state, Bonald's philosophy is the antithesis of the Enlightenment."[7] Taken together, the selections from Bonald's parliamentary oratory demonstrate his principled advocacy of social policies and legislation shaped by a Catholic conception of human nature and society, and prove that he should be recognized as one of the founders of the tradition of Catholic social teaching and action.

Bonald served as a member of parliament throughout the Bourbon Restoration, as an elected deputy until December 1823, and afterward as a member of the upper house, the Chamber of Peers. He was, however, too faithful to his convictions to win favors or a large following under the Restoration, defined as it was by a certain pragmatism. He did play a significant role as a publicist, collaborating with Chateaubriand in the work of France's first and greatest conservative journal of opinion, *Le Conservateur*. During the 1820s, France began to make her first strides toward industrialization, and Bonald spoke more insistently about the dangers this posed to the social order. Indeed, he was one of the first to oppose the uncritical admiration of the English factory system.[8] One of his most pointed critiques of industrialism was his essay "On Political Economy," which appeared in *Le Défenseur*, the short-lived successor to *Le Conservateur*. In 1826, he wrote a long essay comparing the effects of agriculture and industrial production upon the family and calling for the restoration of entail and primogeniture, which may be read elsewhere in English translation.[9] Much of the doctrine of that work is encapsulated in his two essays of 1829 that round out this volume: "On Pauperism" and "On Foundling Children." Bonald had been active in Catholic charitable works in Paris, and he had firsthand knowledge of the sufferings of the urban poor. His essays on the subject neatly tie together our collection, for they combine political and economic reflections with the forceful reiteration of Bonald's defense of the Christian family.

The essays presented in this volume show Bonald to have been essentially a moral reformer. He believed France to have suffered not one but three revolutions in the eighteenth century, beginning under the Regency (1715–1723) with "the revolution of morals," continuing, at mid-century with "the revolution of doctrines," and ending, with the century, "by the revolution of laws."[10] Through these three revolutions, the French nobility had, by turns, abandoned the practice of the virtues, exchanged their Christian convictions for enlightened ones, and, in the Revolution of 1789, been largely responsible for the redefinition of French society in accord with these earlier changes. The social effects of these revolutions had been catastrophic. The family had been abandoned to the free reign of man's unbridled passions with the legalization of divorce in 1792. Local communities and trade guilds had been sacrificed to the pursuit of gain and dissolved in the name of individual property rights. The Church, finally, had been proscribed, persecuted, and plundered. With the Church disappeared the patrimony of the poor, those countless religious orders and institutions of social assistance and moral education that had for centuries done the hard work of civilizing France and ministering to her social ills. Much needed to be done after 1815 to set matters right, and even before the work could begin there would need to be a change of heart on the part of those most gravely responsible: the rich and the former nobility. Bonald labored valiantly and in his own life set a worthy example. He successfully passed on the Faith to his children and spent thirty years attempting to reclaim his land from the Revolutionaries who had cut down all of his trees, like "the Moors [who] left not a single bush in the two Castiles."[11] Unfortunately, his message of self-restraint and dutifulness failed to convert as many of France's former nobles and new rich as he would have liked. An illustration of this sad truth may be seen in the novels of Balzac, himself something of a disciple of Bonald, particularly *Père Goriot* or *Eugénie Grandet*. Balzac's bleak world of rapacious social-climbers and hoary misers wearied by long vigils with their ill-gotten gain is the world whose birth-pangs Bonald had witnessed. Locke, Voltaire, and their ilk had promised worldly happiness to man should he shuck off the dead weight of Christian tradition, aristocratic privilege, and monarchical authority. By the time of Bonald's death in 1840 that promise was daily becoming more difficult to believe.

Bonald's was not, of course, the only voice raised in protest against the social world born of the French and Industrial Revolutions. He was himself indebted to numerous English commentators and critics, chief among them Thomas Malthus, the author of the *Essay on the Principle of Population* (1803). Bonald esteemed Malthus's book, as can be seen in a number of the essays included below, principally for his warning about the danger of overpopulation. Yet Malthus was more than an alarmist; like Bonald, he was a moralist and a critic of the Enlightenment's utopian optimism.

Malthus's own nemesis was William Godwin, an English disciple of Rousseau, but he also contended against the Marquis de Condorcet, one of Bonald's chief foes. In addition to Malthus, Bonald also admired Oliver Goldsmith's "The Deserted Village," and like Goldsmith protested eloquently against the destruction of rural community by the theft of common lands. He did not seem to be aware of the protest against the English factories lodged by Robert Southey, one of England's leading Tory voices, and he looked askance at the Luddites' destructiveness, but he had read a number of other English tracts about the growth of factories and the industrial poor, and seems to have been influenced by Maurice Rubichon's *De l'Angleterre* (1811), a work critical of industrialization, which he recommended and loaned to his friend the Abbé de Lamennais.[12] Finally, Bonald read and found congenial John Lingard's *History of England*, the work that undergirded William Cobbett's claim that the Reformation had been the chief cause of economic revolution and consequent social misery in England.

After Bonald's death, his influence continued to be felt most strongly in conservative and Catholic circles in France, where his works were widely read for the balance of the century. His direct influence was most impressive in the case of his youngest son, Maurice, the Cardinal Archbishop of Lyon from 1840 to 1870, whose annual Lenten pastoral letters show him to have been a stalwart advocate of the poor as well as an insightful analyst of the social ills wrought by the factory system.[13] Balzac considered himself to be a member of Bonald's school and popularized Bonaldian sentiments in his own brand of pithy realism: "When it beheaded Louis XVI, the Revolution beheaded in his person all fathers of families."[14] At the mid-century, the pugnacious ultramontane journalist Louis Veuillot carried on Bonald's protest against the secularization of French society, and Veuillot's ally, the Spanish publicist Juan Donoso Cortes, repeated Bonald's warning that the unchurched industrial poor were tinder in the hands of the socialist revolutionary movement.[15] The sociologist Frédéric Le Play was called "a rejuvenated Bonald" by the literary critic Sainte-Beuve, and although Le Play's thought betrays a fundamental bias in favor of economic liberty that does not accord with Bonald's thinking, his *Social Reform in France* (1864) did call for the restoration of the property-owning family which is as Bonaldian a thesis as may be found.[16] Finally, the labors of René de La Tour du Pin in the last quarter of the nineteenth century extended and deepened Bonald's influence on Catholic social thought. Like Bonald, La Tour du Pin was a landed aristocrat who thought of himself as a "man of tradition." He elaborated a consistent theory of the corporate state in which the common good was understood to be something greater and more worthy than the mere sum of private goods.[17] The tradition of papal social encyclicals was, in turn, strongly shaped by La Tour du Pin's emphasis on the principle of association, or, as it is more commonly known since the social encyclicals of John Paul II, the principle of solidarity.

It is difficult to speak of a direct influence by Bonald in the years after World War I, or in the Catholic world outside of France. It is, however, worth noting that some of the enduring themes readily associated with other writers were adumbrated by Bonald in the essays here collected. In Germany, for instance, the sermons of Wilhelm-Emmanuel von Ketteler during Advent of the momentous year 1848 can be said to have inaugurated the tradition of episcopal social teaching with an essentially Bonaldian emphasis on marriage and family structure as the irreplaceable foundation of a Christian and just society.[18] Later and in England, Hilaire Belloc's warning about the approaching "servile state" finds a precursor in the final paragraph of Bonald's 1810 essay on "The Wealth of Nations." T. S. Eliot's defense of Christian civilization and his forthright calling into question of "the iniquity of usury" points to, if not the influence of Bonald, then at least the fertility of the French conservative tradition to which he gave birth and of which Eliot was a confirmed disciple.[19] Of more recent voices raised in protest against liberal individualism and industrial capitalism, few have been more eloquent than Wendell Berry, and none more penetrating than Alasdair MacIntyre. Neither seems to have been influenced by Bonald in any way, yet the essential harmony of many of their convictions with his is nonetheless striking.

Bonald has suffered from neglect at the hands of historians of Catholic social thinking. Sister Mary Ignatius Ring's study of the Restoration public servant Alban de Villeneuve-Bargemont, for instance, praises its subject for his critique of Adam Smith and his insistence upon the fundamental connection of economics to ethics, but fails to mention Bonald's contribution, even though Bonald was the leading spokesman of conservative Catholic opinion in his day and had championed the same points from the rostrum of the French parliament.[20] An oversight by an economist seeking to bring old theories to the light of day may be readily pardoned, but the silence of professional historians is harder to excuse. Jean-Baptiste Duroselle, Roger Aubert, and, following their analysis, Paul Misner, have all set Bonald on the margins of the development of Catholic social thought, preferring to stress the contributions of political liberals while generally dismissing Bonald and his followers for their reactionary and paternalistic prescriptions.[21] It is telling that Bonald has been better served by historians writing in a Marxist or socialist tradition, as witness one scholar's judgment that Bonald's work displays "an interesting organic critique of the harsh new world of laissez-faire, in which peasant communities and artisanal skills were being destroyed by capitalist greed."[22] The essays in this volume confirm that judgment. They show that Bonald's sight was indeed clear and keen, and that his effort to recall men to the fundamental principles of Christian society was no mere posture of reaction, but part of the timeless message of the Gospel. |•

Notes

[1] Louis de Bonald, "De la Richesse des Nations," *Oeuvres de M. de Bonald* (Bruxelles: Société nationale pour la propagation des bons livres, 1845), VII: 585

[2] Henri de Bonald, *Notice sur M. le Vicomte de Bonald, in Oeuvres,* VIII: 490.

[3] Henri de Bonald, Notice, VIII: 487. The best biographical sketch of Bonald remains Henri de Moulinié, *De Bonald* (Paris: Alcan, 1916). The principal English-language study of his life and work, David Klink's *The French Counterrevolutionary Theorist Louis de Bonald* (New York: Peter Lang, 1996), provides valuable information, but is written from a labored and unsympathetic perspective and is ultimately unsatisfactory.

[4] Bonald, "Notice Historique sur Louis XVI," [1819], in *Oeuvres complètes de M. de Bonald,* ed. J.-P. Migne (Paris: Migne, 1865), III: 891.

[5] Bonald to Madame Victor de Sèze, letter of October 20, 1817, in Henri Moulinié, ed., *Lettres inédites du Vicomte de Bonald à Madame Victor de Sèze* (Paris: Alcan, 1915), 21.

[6] This is the one work of Bonald to have enjoyed a complete English translation: Louis de Bonald, *On Divorce,* trans. Nicholas Davidson (New Brunswick, NJ: Transaction, 1992).

[7] Robert Nisbet, "De Bonald and the Concept of the Social Group," *Journal of the History of Ideas* 5 (1944): 315–31, at 318.

[8] See D. K. Cohen, "The Vicomte de Bonald's Critique of Industrialism," *Journal of Modern History* 41 (1969): 475–84.

[9] "The Agricultural Family, the Industrial Family, and the Right of Primogeniture," in Christopher Olaf Blum, ed., *Critics of the Enlightenment: Readings in the French Counter-Revolutionary Tradition* (Wilmington, DE: ISI Books, 2004), 107–29.

[10] Bonald, "De l'éducation publique," *Le Conservateur* 53 (V; 1819): 19.

[11] Bonald, "Opinion sur l'Article premier du Titre XI du projet de loi de Finances," [March 4, 1817], in *Oeuvres,* VI: 402.

[12] Félicité de Lamennais, *Correspondence générale,* ed. Louis Le Guillou (Paris: Armand Colin, 1971), I: 575.

[13] See Paul Droulers, "Le Cardinal de Bonald et la question ouvrière à Lyon avant 1848," *Revue d'histoire moderne et contemporaine* IV (1957): 281–301.

[14] Balzac, *Maximes et pensées,* ed. Barbey d'Aurevilly, in *Tensions of Order and Freedom: Catholic Political Thought, 1789–1848,* ed. Béla Menczer (1952; New Brunswick, NJ: Transaction, 1994). On Balzac's debts to Bonald, see Ronnie Butler, *Balzac and the French Revolution* (London: Croom Helm, 1983), 260–61.

[15] Selections from Veuillot and Donoso Cortes may be found in Menczer, ed., *Tensions of Order and Freedom.* See also R. A. Herrera, *Donoso Cortes: Cassandra of the Age* (Grand Rapids, MI: Eerdmans, 1995).

[16] See the selections from Le Play in Blum, ed., *Critics of the Enlightenment,* 197–256.

[17] See La Tour du Pin's "On the Corporate Regime," in Blum, ed., *Critics of the Enlightenment,* 315–38.

[18] The text of the sermons may be found in Rupert Ederer, *The Social Teachings of Wilhelm-Emmanuel von Ketteler, Bishop of Mainz* (Lanham, MD: University Press of America, 1977).

[19] T. S. Eliot, "The Idea of a Christian Society" [1939], in Eliot, *Christianity and Culture* (New York: Harcourt, 1977), 20. For Eliot's debts to the French conservative tradition, mediated by the writings of Charles Maurras, see Russell Kirk, *Eliot & His Age: T. S. Eliot's Moral Imagination in the Twentieth Century* (Peru, IL: Sherwood Sudgen, [1971] 1984), 161.

[20] Sister Mary Ignatius Ring, *Villeneuve-Bargemont: Precursor of Modern Social Catholicism, 1784–1850* (Milwaukee: Bruce, 1935).

[21] J.-B. Duroselle, *Les Débuts du Catholicisme social en France (1822–1870)* (Paris: Presses Universitaires de France, 1951). For a collection of Canon Aubert's essays see Aubert, *Catholic Social Teaching: An Historical Perspective,* ed. David A. Boileau (Milwaukee: Marquette University Press, 2003). Paul Misner, *Social Catholicism in Europe: From the Onset of Industrialization to the First World War* (New York: Crossroad, 1991).

[22] Roger Magraw, *France 1815–1914: The Bourgeois Century* (New York: Oxford University Press, 1986), 31.

1 | 1802
The Family in Society

Selections from Primitive Legislation, 1802

THREE KINDS of persons belong exclusively to the domestic condition of society, and, devoted as they are to domestic cares, they cannot exercise public functions. These are women, children, and the people, that is, those who practice the mechanical arts. Theirs is what is called the weakness of sex, of age, and of condition.

The family has needs for its upkeep and sustenance, and to the extent that it is isolated from other families, it is forced to provide for them itself. It constructs its home, prepares its food and clothes, makes its tools and weapons. In the more civilized condition, agricultural families are more industrious to the extent that they inhabit a place set apart from others and can count on less help from their neighbors. This is especially to be seen in the inhabitants of the mountains. Modern administrations, concerned to promote mechanical inventions that make man's work easier and more productive, do not clearly enough perceive that the more machines there are to replace men, the more men there will be in society who are nothing but machines.

The division of labor is introduced with the multiplication of families. Each family devotes itself exclusively to a particular kind of work, initially a necessary one, then one that is useful, finally those that are merely agreeable to the family, and what it does exclusively and habitually it soon does faster and better. Thence arise the domestic professions, also known as the mechanical arts. Agriculture is not a profession, for in its fixed state it is the natural and necessary condition of domestic society, while in its wandering state its natural condition is the hunt. For this reason, agriculture and hunting are equally honorable. The nomadic family, which lies at the mean between the civilized family—the family fixed to the soil—and the family in the savage state, lives from the produce of its flocks. This subsistence is less precarious than that afforded by hunting, but less secure than what man is able to win from the cultivation of fields.

Those who devote themselves exclusively to the domestic professions are in a general condition of domestic dependence, inasmuch as they are at the service of the family and they live by their work and its needs.

Public society also has its needs. It needs public activity continually exercised upon a large number of men in order to rule their wills and their personal actions. In religion, this public activity is called the *cult*, or discipline, and in the State, the *government* or administration. It is, in both societies, the office of those who know the laws and enforce them. Those who *serve* this activity are called *ministers*, from the word *ministrare*, which means to serve. In religion, they are the priests; in the State, the judges and the warriors; and their work or function is called a duty or an *office, officium*, or even a *service*. They are the servants of society, and too often they are treated as her slaves. They judge, they fight, they die for her, and sometimes are killed by her. They are public men, and their distinction, by a strange reversal of conceptions, has seemed, even to them, to be a prerogative, while it is in fact nothing but servitude. "Let he among you who would be first serve the others," said the universal power to his first ministers.

These domestic or public professions are necessary to domestic and public society, and one cannot conceive of the existence of the family without the professions of mason, tailor, and the others that defend the family from the evils of the seasons, anymore than one can conceive of the existence of the State and of religion without the professions of judge and priest, which defend them against the passions of men.

Yet there are some professions that are necessary neither to the family, for they were born long after she was, nor to public society, for they often hasten its degeneration. These are the agreeable arts and the commerce that trades in their products. It is true that these occupations enrich and amuse the family, and that their products lend great brilliance to a State. It is, nevertheless, true that however great a consideration the present revolution has given to these arts and to commerce, blacksmiths remain more necessary to domestic society than painters, and judges more necessary to political society than bankers. It is precisely because these professions were not at bottom necessary, in all the rigor of that word, that they have been injurious, and that after having led society into depravity through corruption and cupidity, they have thrown it into a revolution, by causing the domestic professions to rise up against the public professions, and private men against public men.

What I have said about commerce and the arts can be applied to those sciences other than the social sciences, which are, for religion, theology and morals, and for the State, politics and jurisprudence, that is to say, the science of power and that of duties, which instruct men about their relations with religious and political power and the relations that they have amongst themselves, both as faithful and as citizens.

The physical sciences, which treat the relations of bodies, are highly favored in our day, but will, if we are not careful, change the French nation into a people of geometers and naturalists. They will replace lofty thoughts, generous sentiments, and colorful visions, with their dry axioms and cold and abstract arguments. They are the "infertile pasture of curious and weak minds," as the great Bossuet said, "which, in the end, lead away from that which truly exists," because they are always occupying man with purely material objects, and turning him away from the consideration of his own intelligence, and of the intelligence that governs the universe, that is, the reason for his duties, and the motive for his virtues. These kinds of knowledge—some of which are but dry systems of names or clever calculations—will destroy the most noble arts, the arts of thinking and of feeling, oratory and poetry, the most renowned instruments of instruction, arts that, more than our conquests, have established the incontestable dominion of the French nation in Europe.

The government should therefore rein in the physical or natural sciences and keep them in their place by rendering their results useful to society, by rewarding right practice and preventing abuses, and especially by remembering that public esteem should be proportionate to public utility, and that if the physical sciences observe a nation, the moral sciences alone can civilize it. I know the worth of the mechanical arts and the utility that a wise government can derive from them, and I speak here only of their abuse, and of the need to fix their place and regulate their use.

Let us then distinguish between the private man and the public man, as nature herself has distinguished domestic society from public society.

Public men are those who assist the activity of the power of public society: the priesthood in the Church and the civil magistracy and the military in the State.

All others, working for the family or in the family, are private men. Civilized men have always so highly valued the spiritual part of their being that they have not measured the degree of consideration due to the different professions, even the private ones, upon their real utility, but instead upon the greater or lesser extent of mental study they require and by the products that result from them. It is this that has given the advantage to physicians, architects, and painters over carpenters, bakers, and tailors—although the latter are incomparably more useful. Nothing better proves that all men have some sense of the spirituality of their being than this general opinion about the arrangement of the different professions within society, and it is an odd inconsistency when learned men occupied with sciences requiring great efforts of intelligence persist in seeing man only as organized and sensate matter.

In the same way, in the public professions, the grade is more honorable to the extent that a man's intellect is employed, and this is what makes the condition of the officer more worthy than that of the soldier, and that of the judge more worthy than the prison warden, even though the soldier and the prison warden also directly contribute—and even at the cost of greater effort and the risk of danger—to the activity of the public power.

Yet (and here I beg the reader to take note of how reasonable opinions are formed among men and maintain themselves in spite of men) the domestic and public professions were classified within society, by the sole reason of the greater or lesser spirituality—if I may be allowed the expression—of each of them, and also of the more or less direct service that society derives from them. Thus in the earliest days of the universities, the higher rank among the scholars belonged to theology and to the study of law rather than to medicine and the humanities, just as in the world an architect is thought to be better than a baker and a painter better than a mason.

Yet when in this past century some thought that comic actors should be raised to the rank of public men because they performed for the public, opinion protested against the absurdity. The profession of acting has in fact abased itself all the more in spite of the efforts that have been made to render it honorable, and we may be assured that the opinion that condemns it still exists in all of its force. In fact, because the Revolution brought to light many social truths, we will see more distinctly than we once did that it is noble to devote oneself to the public utility and ignoble to sell oneself to the public's pleasures. This is why the title of public man is an honor, while that of a public woman is an outrage.

One should here note that public instruction in theology has always been in the hands of the ministers of religion, and perhaps one day it will be said that those who have labored with the greatest success in the public law of nations—which is very different from jurisprudence, the private law of families—have been men attached to the public ministry of the State such as Grotius, Pufendorff, and Montesquieu.

The final condition of domesticity is the salary by which a man is made dependent upon another man for his subsistence. The cultivation of the arts, and even of the liberal arts when a profit is gained from it, participates in some regard in this defect of consideration, and even the public man is less public, when he is not a landowner and when he draws a daily wage, because wages are as precarious and variable as the will of man and the course of events. This is, on the contrary, what ennobles the condition of the landowner–cultivator, and that renders it compatible with public professions. For in the past in France a class of men served the State, either in the courts of justice, or in the armies, with the capital of their possessions, as Montesquieu most correctly observed. Different institutions produce different effects, and even if one method may not be lacking in power, it may still be lacking something in dignity.

———— • ————

Domestic education is what the child receives in his family, and it begins at birth.

Man has a mind, a body, and affections, three faculties that depend upon one another in virtue of the laws of their union. These three faculties are to develop concurrently, and one notes in children for whom the development of knowledge or even of their affections precedes by too much their physical growth—whether it is their minds that are prematurely cultivated or their hearts that are too sensitive—that they almost never attain adulthood, and, in general, that those whose physical development is too rapid rarely attain a high degree of instruction or knowledge.

The education of man, at whatever age, should be at once the education of his mind and of his body; yet just as the mind ought not be overloaded with lessons, so also the body should not be burdened with too much attention.

The sophists, and Jean-Jacques Rousseau most especially, who have made all things unnatural by always speaking about nature, have considered only the child's senses. As their metaphysical systems agree that all of our knowledge comes only from the senses, it follows that they labor only to perfect the child's organs of activity, without thinking at all of directing his reason toward objects more capable of extending and ennobling his intelligence. Yet even admitting that the young require a great deal of physical care, we see that these sophists have abandoned civilized man in favor of the brute nature of the animal or of the savage. Thence come all of the practices of the English, the Americans, and our philosophers, practices that are at the very least impractical for the majority of mothers and children. One such method is to immerse the child and bathe his head in cold water, as if man were an animal destined to live in the water or a plant that needed to be watered. We are beginning to abandon all of those strange systems that were invented by the love of paradox and welcomed by a taste for the new. The best minds presently hold that moderate warmth is necessary for the health of children and the development of their organs. Little animals themselves are for a long time warmed by their mothers; and the air, into which man is born and in which he must live, hardens the body just as well as water does, and with less difficulty for the mothers and fewer dangers for the children. Light clothing, an uncovered head, a hard bed, sobriety and exercise, more privations than delights: In a word, what costs less is almost always what best suits us. Nor does nature employ such expense or care to raise up the frail edifice that endures only a few moments and may be blown over in the breeze.

Just as the author of being has spread man throughout the world as the steward of his domain, so nature gives birth to him, and allows him to grow and to live in the most diverse latitudes and the most hostile climates. One does, however, note that civilized people are more numerous and live longer than savage peoples, and that temperate men—all other things being equal—retain their faculties longer than other men. This proves two truths that have been contested by our sophists: the one, that civilization is the perfection of society; the other, that man's perfection includes temperance.

Jean-Jacques Rousseau romanticized the savage condition and denigrated the civilized condition by exalting the bodily vigor, the perfection of the senses, and even the virtues of the uncivilized man. He made savagery fashionable, and soon women—whose weakness disposes them to lend an ear to novelties and whose vanity disposes them to spread them—will raise their children like little Eskimos, troubling themselves only with the development of their limbs and not at all with that of their intelligence.

Yet the sophist of Geneva, who pined for the keenness of vision, the fleetness of foot, and the strength of fibre of the Iroquois, just as he exaggerated their supposed virtues, did not see that these strongest of men are the weakest of peoples, that these tenderest of fathers are the most ferocious of warriors, that these men so hospitable to travelers are pitiless toward their enemies, and that civilized society, on the contrary, though composed of such egotistical men, founds establishments where all of the miseries of humanity are cared for, and in war respects the disarmed enemy as well as the unarmed family. He does not see that this society, formed of such weak, soft men, drives out the savage society as the wind blows the dust, and pushes out to the extremities of the globe these tribes who are given over to the most violent passions and who destroy themselves by their pitiless wars and their unbridled intemperance.

Because the first instrument of our knowledge is language, nature gives to children, and to all children, a singular aptitude to learn and to retain words, the expressions of ideas, which, having entered into their thoughts, give to the mind a consciousness or perception of itself and of its own ideas, just as light penetrating into a dark place gives to our eyes the vision of our own body and the surrounding bodies.

The child learns more or less equally from what is said and what is done in his presence, as from what is said and what is done for him. One must, therefore, greatly respect the eyes and the ears of children: *Maxima debetur puero reverentia* (The child should be held in great reverence).

The first instruction of a child—that instruction of which man is able neither to measure the extent nor evaluate the influence—consists therefore in habits rather than in reasoning, in example much more than in direct lessons, that is to say, in all that he understands rather than in all that he listens to. And for the education of children it is as much a disaster to comport oneself carelessly in their presence as it is to allow them to perceive that one fears too much to be observed.

To the extent that children familiarize themselves with words and consequently with the expression of their ideas, they become more capable of making connections and of receiving the elements of some system of knowledge, or the ensemble of ideas on a given subject. This is the point at which instruction in the public religion should begin; in the early years, and before the age of reason, the child is only a Christian because of the faith of his parents. Yet when he has acquired a sufficient power of reason, he passes into the ranks of the faithful or believers, and before being initiated into the mysteries of Christianity, he receives public instruction from the ministers of religion.

In France there was an excellent institution known as the Brothers of Christian Schools. They should, if possible, be reestablished, for a common education of children is impossible without a common institution of masters.

The question has often been mooted whether it is fitting to give to people the beginnings of a knowledge that they cannot perfect, and, in this question, as in all of those that are connected to pressing interests and important truths, we have fled to the extremes. Some would make all men into philosophers guided by pure reason; others would make them into machines who move only by weights and springs, or animals governed only by the lash. These two extreme opinions have their source in opposing errors. The philosophers, who have read much but observed little, willingly believe in the mind and that there are many men of hidden talents. They think that in order to discover these men of talent it suffices to instruct the people's reason. This, they think, would cause many a Descartes or a Bossuet to spring up, even among the most obscure classes. It is true that men superior to others in knowledge cannot fail to be supremely useful; they are rare, however, because they are less necessary to society than one might think. Society lives according to a hereditary wealth of ancient truths and receives new developments only gradually and to the extent that new needs render them necessary. Men do not invent truths; all they do is derive new consequences from and find new connections among truths long known. Men who are truly superior to others rise up on their own, and, when necessary, push aside every obstacle standing in their way, and they take from the common education a kind of knowledge peculiar to themselves—for if like other men they required the favor of circumstances or the help of a special kind of instruction in order to rise up, they would hardly be superior. Yet as society can never recognize them nor foresee the moment of their appearance, it gives to all, to the extent that it can, the first beginnings of knowledge, from which the greater number derive no profit at all, yet which opens to superior geniuses the career that they are destined to travel.

Those, on the other hand, who, based on false appearances, think that revolutions are born from the progress of enlightenment, mistake the dim glow of lies for the bright light of truth. The truth can never be harmful to man, for it is the truth because it is useful to him. Men suffer only because of their failure to know the truth with a knowledge that is as distinct as the sentiment of their passions is lively and urgent. Great disorders in society have come only from the ignorance of men and the fault of governments, which understood their power no better than their subjects understood their duties. In particular, the present revolution in Europe can be attributed solely to the credulity of governments toward the doctrine of the rights of man and to the impious and senseless dogma of the sovereignty of the people.

And yet—here is a truth that cannot be too much insisted upon— everything is relative in society, for society itself is but an ensemble of relations and connections. If the governments were to establish schools where the children of the people might learn to read, and thus become susceptible to receiving the most deadly errors as well as the most useful truths, they should then allow only the circulation of good books, which are always few in number in each subject, and they should cleave to this principle: A people that reads much requires few books.

Nor is it inopportune to note that the Christian religion, which has been accused of perpetuating ignorance, has been the cause of the spread of the art of reading amongst the people, whom she has invited to join in the public prayers and the chant of the ministers of religion. Under this heading the Brothers' schools are to be included.

Governments, so keen to propagate the knowledge of new agricultural processes or the discoveries of the mechanical arts, have been much less concerned to spread the works fitting for the domestic instruction of the people's children. Philosophy has taken up the charge, and has labored at it with ardor and perseverance. Meanwhile the ministers of religion did not sufficiently realize—or at least did not generally realize—that the dry repetition of a highly abridged catechism no longer satisfied the liveliness and the penetration of the French nation. When the fundamental social truths of *power* and *duty* were loudly attacked with the whole art of sophistry, it was necessary to give justifications of their credibility to the faithful. This instruction, however exalted it may appear to be, is within the grasp of all men because it is most natural to their minds. In it they find the explanation of their own domestic relations, where, just as in the religious or political society, all is but *power* and *duty*.

Moreover, let it not be thought that it is absolutely necessary for the happiness and well-being of a people that it know how to read and to write. This knowledge is not even necessary for its interests; and society needs a more effective guarantee against the bad faith of those with whom it has to contend. Good laws and a firm and vigilant government: This is what all men need, and *all the rest shall be added unto them.*

Children, in growing up in the bosom of the family, form themselves insensibly to the mind and the practice of the paternal profession, for which they have so powerful a taste, born from their first objects, their first examples, and their first habits. This truth, so fruitful in administration, applies equally to the family devoted to domestic labors and even to the family devoted to the more noble cares of public ministry. It is in this natural disposition of man to contract from his infancy the habits that he will retain throughout his life that is found the reason for the heredity of professions, without which a society cannot long endure and which assures the perpetuity of the most base and dangerous crafts as well as of the most honorable functions. This heredity was common to the peoples who have left behind them monuments of their time upon the earth: the

Hebrews, the Egyptians, and the Romans—and especially the Romans, from whom we have taken everything, except what was severe in their morals and wise in their laws.

As nature ranks men by families, society should rank families by corporate bodies or guilds, and one would hardly believe the force with which families of the same professions tend to form corporate bodies. This corporate spirit is to be seen even in the most base crafts. Thence the guilds of the mechanical professions, known under the name of the *jurandes* (sworn memberships) or the *maîtrises* (master-ships), existed in every Christian State. Philosophy, that universal solvent, relentlessly pursued their destruction under the vain pretext of a competition that profited neither the honest merchant, nor the arts themselves, nor the purchasers. These guilds, in which religion strengthened the regulations of the civil authority, had, among other advantages, that of containing by the stern power of the masters the rudeness of a youth that had been sent abroad from the paternal power at a young age by the necessity to earn its keep, yet was too obscure to be watched over by the political power. A child of the people who traveled around France to become instructed in his craft was provided by his master with a certificate and could find work anywhere, as well as something still more precious: someone to watch over him. And I say from familiarity with the cause that no political institution exists that an attentive administration might employ to greater advantage to form the morals of the people and even to add to the people's ease.

The enemy of man, who always sows the tares amidst the good grain, set these guilds in opposition to one another, and sometimes divided them against themselves by the activities of two Masonic organizations known as the *Gaveaux* and the *Compagnons du Devoir*,* which were constantly at war with one another and more bitterly opposed than the Hurons and the Algonquins. The administration—which did occasionally wake up—made some vain efforts to stamp out these associations, useless as they were to the progress of the arts, and whose first law was to assist the brothers and to grow in membership. When governments will have understood this truth,

---

* EDITOR'S NOTE: The names of the two Masonic groups are somewhat obscure. Compagnons du Devoir suggests "Dutiful Journeymen" or "Brothers of Duty," while Gaveaux seems to derive from the verb *gaver*, to force-feed a goose.

they should use public force to prevent the activity of these groups. I hope they will be moved by a profound sentiment of justice, which, like the goodness of God, is appeased only after the punishment. When at last they have the will—for it is rare that they are of one will—to work in concert with the authority of religion (more effective than political authority against these occult institutions—of which there are far more dangerous ones than these), they will restore those possessed by these private and disordered affections to a more general benevolence. With firmness and with time—that first minister of all legitimate authority and the irresistible tool of every useful institution—the governments will work marvels. "If we were sufficiently fortunate," said Leibniz, "to one day have a great monarch who would want to take to heart the means of increasing in us the knowledge of the good and the natural light of the Divinity, we would do more for the happiness of mankind in ten years than one could otherwise do in several centuries."

The guilds also have the advantage of uniting men whom fortune and condition condemn to obscurity and of giving them both consideration and importance by their union. I believe that the great lords in Flanders used to seek the honor of admission to a guild of merchants or artisans, and I am not sure that there were not great advantages to this custom, both for the patrons and for the clients. What we have said about civil corporations applies just as well to religious ones or to confraternities, which can be maintained when they have a useful object, but which should be subjected to a wise rule, for fear that they will not so rule themselves.

The government should regard the condition of the journeyman as the domestic education of the people's children. For the interest of the young people themselves, great authority must be given to the masters, so that they will abuse it less. The laws that used to obtain in France should be restored, for they were perfect on this point, as they were on all others. Yet if there was strength in the laws, there was weakness in men. Religion thundered in vain in the ears of the kings; in vain, for to arouse their vigilance, she showed them man, inclined toward disorder and a rebel from his very birth. A soft and unmanly philosophy invited them to slumber, repeating to them over and over again that men are naturally good; yet these men who were so good did not have much regard for authority unless it made itself feared, and the disdain of the people for subordinate authorities—which appeared to them to be far more concerned to collect taxes and to order public works than to prevent or to correct disorders—led insensibly to the weakening and the fall of the highest authorities.

It is an intolerable abuse for children to be left wandering around, in a veritable school for corruption and thievery. Professional beggars, and especially the blind ones, travel around from town to town with a train of children of both sexes, hoping to spur commiseration with their lot, and these children are thus raised without checks, without instruction, and having under their eyes only the example of laziness, and in their hearts only the appetites of the needy, and in their mouths only the supplications of lowliness and even at times the ruses of the impostor. The first duty of the government is to prevent this disorder by every means of assistance, and, if necessary, of vigor, that it has at its disposal. It owes a more vigilant protection to the poorest families, and if it cannot prevent the old men and the lame from begging, it at least should not allow anyone to live as vagabonds. Vagrancy in the State is like those peccant humours in the human body, which cause trouble in all of its functions and which must be fixed in one place when they cannot be entirely purged. If the government should prohibit vagrancy to children, even when they are begging on behalf of their parents, still less should it allow greedy parents to make use of the deformities of their children as an object of public curiosity. The humanity, morals, and regard due to those of weak imaginations and to expectant mothers all cry out against a practice that is unworthy of a Christian people. The administration should ensure that lucrative speculation upon misery never be allowed to establish itself.

I have not spoken of the education proper to the various arts that the students receive in their public courses. The authority should watch carefully to ensure that the youth learn only what is useful, and that it not be given lessons in materialism during lectures on medicine, nor be schooled in sensuality by the models they paint. |•

2 | 1806
Political Reflections on Money and Lending at Interest

THE QUESTION of lending at interest was, like so many others, answered long ago in France by our religion and in our politics. If greed made bold to break the law, our tribunals kept watch to suppress it, and public opinion was poised to censure it. While crimes more directly injurious to the public order met only with punishment and, even on the scaffold, preserved a kind of grandeur springing from the principle that had produced them, the crime of usury—that fruit of a vile and base passion—met with material punishment only occasionally, but was, in Europe's most disinterested nation, punished by infamy and ridiculed on the stage. Different times, a different spirit! Our fathers understood neither man nor society. Their wisdom was folly, their virtue a lack of sophistication, their learning ignorance, their experience prejudice. Everything in France, religious precepts, political maxims, laws, customs, honor, even honesty, was called into question. Mankind seemed to begin again, and society as a whole was an unknown to be sought in the unhealthy abstractions of our political algebraists. The question of the nature of money and of its use became the object of lively debate, and soon, when upright men had been outlawed as a dangerous faction, usury came to be regarded as a legitimate practice.

The torrent of new opinions carried all before it. As soon as statesmen and political writers had misunderstood the political reasons behind the religious maxims, it was the turn of weak theologians to misunderstand the religious motives behind the civil laws, and they waffled back and forth between the new doctrine and the old principles. Meanwhile the government, facing the appalling task of making good laws out of bad customs, was obliged to grant complete liberty to freely contracted interest at the same time as it fixed the legal rate of interest.

It must be admitted that the severe Christian doctrine on lending at interest may not have always been defended by entirely satisfactory arguments. The philosophical tolerance of usury, however, has led to intolerable disorders. If once the law's severity was the subject of complaint, it is its leniency that now raises the hue and cry. The government has heard and responded. Our discussions have begun, and this is an unequivocal proof that there is something still to be clarified on this subject, for when the truth has been revealed in all its aspects, the combat between opinions comes to an end, the trial is terminated, and the dispute is struck from the long list of human quarrels.

It is with good reason that the author of a recent work on lending at interest compares the toleration of usury to the toleration of divorce.

Religion, knowing her children and the inexhaustible depths of inconstancy and greed that dwell in their hearts, confided the well-being of man to the repressive force of society and placed as insurmountable barriers before his passions the prohibitions of divorce and of lending at interest without legitimate cause. A shallow philosophy regarding society as a stage on which men gather for their pleasure, or as a house of commerce in which they associate to gain fortunes through speculation, conceded divorce to our sensuousness and usury to our passion for riches. It believed that man's natural reason would hold him fast upon the steep slope of tolerance, and that the people would maintain strong customs in spite of weak laws. Vain hope! The tolerance of divorce became a veritable polygamy, the toleration of lending at interest the most unbridled speculation. It has already become necessary to restrict the permission of divorce to narrow limits, and soon it will become indispensable to build up levees against the furies of usury. So do they fade away, those vain systems founded upon the belief in man's natural goodness and that it is by giving way to man's desires that his passions are kept in check. Thus is justified in all her ways the wisdom of the Christian religion and the severity of her maxims about the terrible corruption of the human heart and the necessity of smothering its desires in order to stymie its passions, to command man to abstain in order to force him to control himself. We must then, at pain of seeing society dissolve and the moral world fall back into chaos, return to the holy and austere laws that once created society and alone are able to preserve it. A little while longer and we may return to them in many other ways. In vain will we quail before them in our weakness, for we will submit, when we must, to the salutary yoke: A people is capable of receiving everything when it has the patience to endure.

When we treat lending at interest in its connections with politics, by which I mean, when we seek the public or political motives for the religious teachings, a swarm of questions rises up. Light must be shed upon all of them, for darkness has been spread abroad, and we must rediscover the elements, because the principles have been misunderstood and disfigured.

What is money? Does money bear interest according to its nature? Is there a natural justification for the rate of interest, or is that rate left to the will of men and to circumstance? Should rates of interest higher than the legal rate of interest be permitted? Finally, in what circumstances and under what conditions may one lend at the legal rate of interest?

The greatest concerns of society, and the most pressing duties of morals depend upon the answers to these questions. They cannot be left undecided. Passions will trespass wherever the law does not dare to pronounce.

What is Money?

Everything comes from the land, just as everything returns to it. This is the most certain principle of political economy, because it is nature's most constant decree. It is always to moral or physical nature that we must return whenever the laws of society or the needs of man are in question.

Whether the people be farmers or traders, whether they be landowners or owners of money, whether they live by the products of their wits or the labor of their bodies, they are fed by the land and the produce of the land that they consume, after they have obtained it through its cultivation. This truth is a fact and a fixed foundation for reasoning—what Leibniz would have called an establishment—from which we may confidently go forward, an axiom that we may leave behind us but never lose sight of, even while we follow the innumerable detours and the infinite variety of human transactions and are furthest removed from it.

If men could exchange at ease the goods they have for those they lack, or goods for the services they require from their fellows, money would be useless, and metals would never have been coined.

But because these exchanges of goods for services, or for goods of differing quality, weight, and volume, are greatly multiplied among advanced peoples, and vary as do their needs, and because these kinds of exchanges are difficult, litigious, and impractical, men sought an easier way of evaluating all sorts of goods and services with a common measure that would signify the value of all kinds of goods and services and that might serve as a prompt and easy means of exchange.

This common and fictitious measure, which bore different names in different lands, was, in France, a piece of silver which the public authority denominated the *franc* and marked with its seal, and which it gives as a sign of the value of every kind of service rendered to the State, and receives as a sign of the value of goods or taxes that it requires of its subjects.

The silver franc is, therefore, in France the universal means of exchange because it is the public and legal sign of every value.

I value at a hundred francs a certain quantity of wheat, and my neighbor values at seventy francs a certain quantity of wine, and I truly and effectively exchange my wheat for his wine in selling him my wheat for a hundred francs while purchasing his wine for seventy.

In the same way a worker exchanges his labor for goods, by valuing his day at two francs and by procuring his daily needs with this money.

It is immediately apparent that one might use as a sign of value and means of exchange any sort of thing other than metal, and that one might not even use any at all and trade merely by bartering goods for goods or goods for services.

In this way small farmers in the countryside often barter wheat for wine. It is in wheat that they pay the blacksmith and the farrier for their handiwork. They pay their shepherds, butlers, and servants in sheep from their flock or even in thread or cloth, and, almost everywhere in the countryside they pay the miller in wheat. Thus in the early days, beasts, whether cattle or sheep (*pecus*, whence pecuniary) were the signs of value and the means of exchange. To the same end, according to Adam Smith, salt was used in Abyssinia, shells on some parts of the coast of India, dried cod in Newfoundland, tobacco in Virginia, sugar, skins, tanned hides in different lands, and even nails in some mountain villages of Scotland. I even believe that in certain countries of Africa or Asia a purely fictional sign is used, that is to say a simple denomination, that takes the place of a common measure and is neither realized nor represented in any manner or by any material object, as if in England the word sterling might be used in the absence of coins.

The reasons that made men adopt and prefer metals to all other materials are known to all.

Coined metals, I repeat, are not therefore considered as having their own proper value in each particular society or according to their intrinsic value. Instead they fulfill the unique office of a legal and public sign of all value and common means of exchange among all goods.

One does not nourish oneself or clothe oneself with gold or silver; one does not build houses of gold or silver; but with money, one procures all that is necessary to nourish, clothe, and lodge oneself. These are the first and only natural needs of the physical man, who has so imprudently burdened himself with secondary and artificial needs, like an ill-advised traveler on a short journey who weighs down his fragile vessel with useless baggage that he must throw into the sea at the first gust of wind.

Coined money, therefore, fulfills in society the role that tokens fulfill in gambling. I beg the reader to reflect upon the comparison with me.

In gambling, money is the good of which the tokens are the sign; and in society, all the products of the land or industry are the goods of which money is the sign.

One may begin with more or less money, or even without money and by bartering goods; just as one may play with a greater or lesser number of tokens, and even without tokens or money upon the table.

According to the number of tokens at play, the same token represents more or less money; and in the same way, according to the amount of money in society, the same sum of money signifies or represents more or less goods.

Too many or too few tokens makes the game difficult to play; too much or too little money makes commerce difficult and exchanges inconvenient.

If there are not enough tokens to play the game, more of them may be made, whether of gold, silver, mother-of-pearl, or ivory. At times they are even made with cards cut after the fashion of tokens. And if there is not enough silver in society, marked paper takes the place of money.

To avoid the inconvenience of having too many tokens, they are reduced to notes or contracts, which represent a certain number of tokens, and sometimes only the points are written down. In the same way to avoid the inconvenience of too great a number of franc coins, they are reduced into écus of three francs, five francs, into pieces of gold of ten, twenty, or forty francs and, finally, into bank papers of five hundred and a thousand francs.

Paper money is, therefore, the sign of a certain quantity of goods, and bank papers of a certain quantity of money. In this latter form, it is the sign of the largest values and the means of the largest exchanges.

In the ordinary condition of things, therefore, paper money makes up for a scarcity of coinage, while bank papers make up for its overabundance.

Yet if, with paper money, one cannot purchase goods for oneself, or if, with bank paper, one cannot obtain a quantity of money at will, then there would be an administrative defect and a principle of ruin in the State. In the same way there would be fraud or violence in a game if a player could not at its end convert the notes, contracts, and tokens he has in front of him into money.

Men of the same country trade among themselves by means of money. People more distant from one another trade together by an exchange of goods. Thus France exports wine, oil, salt, and industrial products; Sweden, iron and copper; Russia, hemp and tar; Italy, silk; Africa, grain; and so on. Yet as these exchanges of different goods, effected at great distances and by different routes and different commercial concerns, cannot ever be complete or definitive—for one people sends more and another less, one sooner the other later, more at one time and less at another—it is necessary for the solvency of these exchanges and the setting right of accounts to cause money to pass from one country to another with a minimum of risk and expense. This is the original purpose and fundamental justification of the commerce of banks considered in general: A purpose disguised under other services, and upon which a wise art has cast the veil of a mysterious language, but which, in the final analysis, and reduced to its most simple expression, is but the means of allowing money to travel with security, ease, promptness, and efficiency from one country to another, for the paying of accounts, and for observing the different monetary values used in the different countries.

Two merchants of the same town can trade with one another without the mediation of a banker, but bankers are required between the merchants of Paris and those of Lyon, and still more between the merchants of France and of Sweden.

It must, however, be noted that what we have said about the original and essential object of the bank is rigorously true only when money is considered solely as a sign of value and means of exchange, for if money is regarded as having a value itself and as merchandise, then banks would have another purpose, or rather they would add another service to their original service: And they should be regarded as shops for buying money, where one would go to purchase this good at a higher or lower price according to the circumstances.

We will consider elsewhere whether money can be thought of as a kind of merchandise.

To summarize: Coined money is a sign of value and a means of exchange. It fulfills in society the function of a sign. It is regarded as a sign by governments, and to them alone, as an attribute of their policing power and as a duty of sovereignty, belongs the right to invest it with the character of public and legal sign of value.

Is It of the Nature of Money to Bear Interest?

Yes and no, according to whether it is used as a sign of naturally productive values, or as the sign of dead values that naturally produce no revenue at all.

In this distinction, founded upon the nature and the very necessity of things, is the reason for our former religious maxims upon usury and our former civil laws upon lending at interest.

The land is a value that is naturally productive, either by producing spontaneously what is necessary to the subsistence of man in his savage state and to that of the animals that nourish a pastoral people, or by producing, partly spontaneously and partly with the assistance of man, what is required by agricultural man and the animals who assist him in his works.

The products of the earth, whether spontaneous or obtained by agriculture, are dead values, values that must be consumed, and which, far from accumulating, will diminish in quantity or in quality when they are kept beyond the time fixed for their maturity. They are also liable to be destroyed by accidents.

Thus I employ a sign to obtain a plot of land, or, to speak in everyday language, I buy a farm. It annually produces a certain quantity of goods, or a revenue. My money has, therefore, produced a real growth of goods, or a revenue.

If I lend this land, stipulating the cost of the lease, then I am in effect exchanging the annual produce of the land for an agreed sum of money. The money originally employed in the acquisition of this land, therefore, naturally brings me a revenue, and when this is converted into money it is called interest.

I lend my neighbor the money for the acquisition of land that is to be reimbursed, that is to say that I really purchase it in whole or in part under the name of another, who reserves the right to buy it back from me. In this case my money can legitimately produce interest for me, because the land naturally produces a revenue.

I use the money to purchase grain for my subsistence. The grain is a dead value that, far from growing, diminishes. Thus in this case my money produces no interest for me.

I lend to another grain for his consumption, or the money to purchase it. This grain produces no increase for him. Thus my money should not produce any interest for me; all that I can require from him is the same sum of money or of grain.

These are the general principles. We will not now trouble ourselves with the exceptions.

Here I will dare—even while treating of the commerce in money—to hold a different opinion than that of Necker.*

"The first one," said the famous administrator, in his *On the Administration of Finances*, "who by prudence or avarice, wished to exchange one part of the produce of his land or labor against a small future increase in revenue, invented the idea that we now call the interest of money. These transactions would have even preceded the introduction of money, because

---

* EDITOR'S NOTE: Jacques Necker (1732–1804), a Swiss Protestant financier, was a minister of state to Louis XVI of France.

when the cultivator who needed a hundred measures of grain to sow his field had to seek them from one who had an excess quantity of them, the idea of paying an annual charge in exchange for the advance presented itself naturally. This very simple manner of joining the convenience of lenders with that of borrowers multiplied the means of labor, and doubtless contributed efficaciously to the general activity that has now spread into every society." I believe that Necker credited the earliest times of societies with agreements that could only have come about in a very advanced society. Nor was it among agricultural people that the first ideas about lending at interest must have grown up. A prudence consisting in foreseeing hypothetical needs amidst satisfied ones, and famine amidst abundance is not the first virtue of primitive man, nor was avarice his first vice. The one who, having an excess quantity of grain that he watched rot in spite of his care, and lent it to his neighbor that he might sow his fields with it, surely did not require that he be rendered a great quantity in return. If in need, he doubtless would have asked his neighbor for reciprocal help and services; yet that he would have in advance made a condition stands against every idea that history has transmitted to us of the first men, as well as all of the ideas of their character and relations that our present knowledge of people living in a savage condition today. Men in innocence, or, if you will, the unrefined state of their first customs and the simplicity of their first ideas, limited in their commerce to the barter of goods for goods or services for services (for Necker supposes that the usage of money might not yet have been introduced) did not think of making fruitful a product that was by necessity unproductive, nor placing a tax to their own profit upon the industry of their fellow man or upon their neighbor's land. Nor would they have done what a man of delicate conscience would not allow himself to do today, amidst all the needs of luxury and the stratagems of greed, and what both laws and customs would prohibit in a few years. Nor is "this manner of joining the convenience of lenders and of borrowers" as simple or as naturally present to the mind as Necker thinks. It is always very complex and supposes many subtle arguments, or rather many sophistries. And as to this general activity that has spread throughout all societies, I believe that Necker would have considered it under another point of view and that he would have distinguished between that activity of mind that is a principle of life and that agitation of the passions that is a forerunner of death if, instead of treating of the administration of the finances of a nation, he had treated of its morals and of its virtues.

Yet if the principle of the commerce of money advanced by Necker is false, what should we think about the theory founded entirely upon this principle?

Money can, therefore, legitimately produce interest when it is employed as a sign to acquire naturally productive values.

Money should not produce interest when it is employed to acquire values that are naturally unproductive.

Yet there are men who purchase unproductive goods in order to sell them to those who lack them, either in their natural condition or transformed by industry into new goods destined to satisfy new needs. This is what is called trade, or commerce properly so called: trade among men near at hand and with the goods of their own lands; commerce among men far apart from one another or with merchandise foreign to the lands in which they inhabit.

The labor of men who purchase, transport, store, preserve, and improve goods merits a salary. The natural decrease, the accidental and eventual loss of goods, and the inevitable waste that they suffer from their transformation into industrial values all require compensation.

This legitimate salary on the one hand, and the natural compensation on the other, are the justification for the legitimate profits of the trade in goods, even those by nature unproductive.

Thus the money employed in land naturally produces interest because the land naturally produces a revenue. And the money employed in commerce legitimately produces a profit, because commerce consists in the labors of the man who merits a salary employed upon values the decrease of which requires compensation.

The annual interest of money employed in the land can be determined and fixed, because within a given time the land produces constantly, annually, and even regularly.

The profit of money employed in commerce can neither be determined nor fixed, because the profits of commerce are variable, uncertain, periodic, and often absolutely nil. Commerce, moreover, occasionally results in losses.

The distinction between interest, which is fixed, and profits, which are variable, is real and important. These two words express two different ideas, and the confusion of these words and ideas upon this subject has been the source of false reasoning in morals and false decisions in politics.

Here is the whole mystery of the two famous axioms of the schools, *lucrum cessans* and *damnum emergens,* which contain the whole doctrine of religion upon the use of money, and the conditions under which our former laws permitted loans to be made at a profit. For if I do not gain interest from money lent for the acquisition of lands naturally producing a revenue, there is *lucrum cessans,* the absence of a natural profit; and if I do not gain a just compensation for money placed in commerce composed of salaries and losses, there is *damnum emergens,* that is to say, imminent danger.

What Should Be the Annual Rate of Interest?

As close as possible to the same as the percentage of annual revenue from land.

This proposition follows naturally from the principles we have laid down.

If money is the sign of productive value, then interest, or the increase of money, should be the sign of the production or the increase of this value.

This rate is taken from the nature of things: It is, therefore, reasonable. It is fixed. It may, therefore, be legal, by which I mean the object of a law.

On the contrary, the interest of money cannot be fixed according to the profits of commerce, because these profits are not naturally fixed, because they often change into real losses, and because one cannot make a positive determination of a value that may eventually be negative.

Now, in considering the produce of the land in France, and in all of her provinces taken together, in compensating for the sterility of some by the fertility of others, the low price of farm labor in some areas by the dearness of it in others, the irregularity of some harvests by the regularity of others, and bad years by good ones, one may conclude approximately and in general that from four to five per cent, or the twentieth or twenty-fifth part of the capital, is the percentage produced by land, with a deduction made of advances, labor, fees, accidents, and waste. This is, however, an approximation because, as farmers know, it is impossible to fix with precision the net produce of small farms.

This percentage of the revenue of the land is acknowledged by landowners, inasmuch as it serves as the ordinary basis for the acquisition of land by mutual agreement; and it seems to be recognized by the government, which takes in its land tax just about the same proportion as the lands produce in revenue.

If the lands cultivated by tenant farmers bring a bit less to the landowner, the lands cultivated by the landowner himself produce a bit more. This is what reestablishes the equilibrium among the produce of all lands taken together.

I am not at all sure whether the legitimate profits of an honest and well-ordered commerce should rise above five per cent of the investment, taking into account all of its operations in a land such as France and all of its profits and losses. In order to decide this question one must know whether a company would double after twenty years the initial investment of a number of investors who would have separately done only marginal business during the same time. I say business, and not brigandage, in which ten times a year one plays at heads or tails with one's own fortune and that of others.

If the profits of commerce regularly rise far above the revenue of the land, it would be a wise measure to bring them back to equality, either by favoring the cultivation of the earth in every possible way, or by containing the speculations of commerce within the limits of general utility. Otherwise commerce will take the lead over landed property, and the businessman will be more politically imposing than the landowner. The land will be abandoned for the cash register, and money, exclusively reserved for mercantile enterprises, will no longer give life to agriculture, the first and noble occupation of man, the nourishing mother of mankind, and the foundation of every resource and every virtue of society.[1]

It would therefore be contrary to the nature of things, and consequently contrary to the interest of society, if where the soil produces annually for the landowner only a twentieth, money were to return a tenth, a fifth, or a quarter.

The government, therefore, should not allow interest to rise above the legal rate, but it should always let it fall below it. The more that landed property holds an advantage over the possession of money, and the more the condition of the landowner is esteemed and sought after, the more one seeks to pass from the mobile condition of the capitalist to the fixed and secure condition of the landowner.

I do not here examine whether governments have always taken the presumed produce of the earth for the basis of the interest paid on money, because I am seeking principles rather than discussing examples. I am speaking of the ordinary and regular circumstances to which governments ought to attend, and not of extraordinary and revolutionary circumstances into which they may be thrown by the course of events.

One should, moreover, never lose sight of the fact that the calculations of political economy do not admit of geometric precision. In the science of numbers and extension, as in every physical science, one separates objects in order to count them one by one, or measure them inch by inch; and the largest operations of arithmetic or practical geometry are never anything other than the addition of units. Yet in the science of society, which is a moral science, with the moral being as its necessary element, one must set aside individuals in order to work with the commonality. Moral theories are true with a general kind of truth; moral practice attains only a moral certitude. One must also take care to distinguish abstractions, which are generalizations applying to nothing, from morals, which are generalizations that apply to everything.[2]

What is Usury?

We come at last to the question of usury, whether one consider it to be interest exceeding the legal rate, or as profit exceeding the limits of legitimacy.

One who lends at ten, twenty, or thirty per cent for another to purchase a landed property that at most yields five per cent; one who lends at any rate of interest whatsoever goods destined only for consumption by the borrower, and which far from yielding revenue, are destroyed in their use; one who derives a profit from money lent for commerce in which the profits were less than the interest exacted: All of these, I say, are unjust men who, without running any risk or performing any labor, desire the earth to produce for them, and for them alone, two, three, and four times more than it produces for the one who cultivates it by the sweat of his brow and runs the risk of loss. Such a one wants products that are unproductive both in their nature and to their consumers to be fruitful for them alone. They wish, finally, to derive a profit from the ruin of their debtor, and even to profit upon his misfortune. This is the religious and political crime of usury, considered as a crime by Domat and Pothier* as well as by Bossuet, and it was punished by our ancient courts of justice, which is to say by the most enlightened tribunals of the world, known for their probity and dignity. This is the *quaestuosa segnitia*, or lucrative idleness, as Pliny the Elder calls it, or murder, to use Cato's words.[3] The usurer, considered from this point of view, is a tyrant who torments nature and humanity.

Thus the landowner who earns five per cent but must pay twenty, the consumer who derives no profit but must pay heavily, and the merchant who must endure his losses alone while the lender makes a profit: All of these must spend down their capital in order to cover the excessive charges of interest. The entire ruin of agriculture and farmers, commerce and merchants, is the infallible consequence of such operations.

The landowner forced to borrow is ruined much sooner if the interest, instead of being stipulated in money, is negotiated in goods. This kind of loan is extremely common today, and it is one of the most cruel vexations that the cities can exert upon the countryside that nourishes them.

The ruin of the borrower is still quicker if the interest, instead of being payed at the end of the agreed-upon term, is paid in advance and retained upon the capital that is lent, because then the borrower shoulders the interest on the interest. This manner of lending is a subterfuge that the lenders use to disguise their exactions, a subterfuge all the more culpable because it gives the appearance of a free loan to the most revolting usury.

Yet greed, in order to escape its consequences, denies the principle, and would have money regarded as merchandise, and subject like any other to all the variations of price that are born from scarcity and abundance. This opinion, which would have appeared monstrous in the past, has been advanced by writers with a great reputation, adopted by respected statesmen, and, like every new opinion, made its fortune in the last century.

Gold and silver would doubtless be merchandise if, like iron or precious stones, they were used only in works of handicraft and skill. Yet as their use

---

* EDITOR'S NOTE: Jean Domat (1625–1696) and Robert Joseph Pothier (1699–1772) were celebrated French jurists.

in precious objects is purely an accessory to their primary use as the sign of value, and as the quantity of coined metals is infinitely greater than that of handcrafted metals, one cannot treat metal coins in the same way that one treats handcrafted metals without upsetting every commercial relation. Another inconsistency of the system that I am opposing is that the metal-matter has a price much more fixed than that of the metal-sign, for an ounce of gold or silver has a certain price that varies little in trade, while the interest paid on money varies from five up to thirty per cent, and even higher.

The sale of this merchandise does not resemble the sale of ordinary goods. In ordinary sales, the whole and entire ownership of the thing sold passes to the buyer in return for a price that he pays but once. In the case of a loan, the property remains with the seller, inasmuch as the thing sold comes back to him with an annual increase that is said to be the price of the sale, even though it only represents a small part of the thing sold, the fifth part, the tenth, or the twentieth. The seller hands over without giving; the buyer receives without keeping. Ordinary goods are sold to every man who pays for them, and sometimes more dearly to the rich than to the poor. Money, on the other hand, is said to be sold, but is never paid for, and is always sold more dearly to the poor than to the rich, because the lender calculates his profits based on the risk that he runs, which is always greater in the case of a debtor in difficult straights. While the millionaire finds money at six or seven per cent per year in Lyon or Bordeaux, the trader in a small town, or the landowner in the countryside, cannot obtain it for less than one and a half or two per cent per month. Money can be had more cheaply by the rich than by those who need it.

What, finally, is this kind of merchandise that no one buys and that everyone wishes to sell? Only the government buys the material of gold or silver in order to make money with it and to mark it with its seal; but it buys it with the money that it provides to its subjects, for it has none other at hand. It is made in its mints, which are public property, by workers whose salaries are paid from the taxes it levies. The State as a body, which comprehends every individual, has therefore bought the metal and paid for the cost of coinage. Once the money is made, the government does not sell it. On the contrary, it uses it to buy what it needs and to pay for services rendered to the State, either in the Church, the courts, the army, or the administration. Those who receive it in this way then use it to pay for the things and the services that they require. The money, flowing from the public treasury as from its source, spreads out like life-giving water to even the smallest channels of general circulation. Everyone has received money as a sign; everyone should give money as a sign. We may say of it: *Gratis accepistis, gratis date* (Freely you have received; now freely give). Money should pass from subject to subject in the same way that it has passed from the prince to the subject. And, I dare say, the crime of denaturing the principle of money is as great, and much more dangerous, than the justly punished crime of counterfeiting the seal or altering the weight of a coin. But if the government has paid the cost of purchasing the metal and making the coins from the taxes paid by the body of its subjects, then we have all bought it once. To sell to the borrower at retail what he already bought at wholesale; to sell something that one did not purchase to those who have already paid for it; to sell to each what belongs to all, and what especially belongs to the body of society: This is a kind of political simony that no sophistry can disguise and that no consideration can excuse.

I return to the comparison of money to tokens. The government that buys metal in order to make the signs of value that would facilitate commerce among its subjects is like the owner of a casino who purchases the tokens in order to make them available for the game, with this difference: The players do not pay for the tokens, while the subjects, in the last analysis, have paid for the money. Yet if it is a custom in a casino to have the players pay for the use of the tokens, as they pay for the use of cards, the players would be obliged to increase the stakes of their game in order to cover the cost of the tokens and cards, or they may play only for the cost of the tokens and cards, in which case all the profits of the game, and all the losses of the players, will be collected by the owner of the casino. In the same way, if it were necessary to begin by purchasing the sign that serves for the exchange of goods, the price of goods would increase in order to cover the cost of the money. It would increase to the pure loss of the seller and the consumer, and all the profits of commerce, all the work of the cultivator, would be to the sole profit of the lender, or rather the seller of money.

When money is no longer the sign of value and a means of exchange between goods, but a value and a good itself, we must beware lest the goods themselves become nothing other than a sign of the value of money and a means of exchange of money. This is what was discovered in France and especially in Paris in the days of the *maximum*,* when with fictional quantities of all kinds of merchandise, quantities that nowhere existed, people bought the money then current, the *assignats*, and with these the few coins still in circulation. This effect is less sensible today, but it is no less real, wherever coined money, turned from its natural office as sign and means of exchange between goods, because itself a commodity and the dearest one of all.

When money is only the sign of values in land, products, and services, then prices rise or fall insensibly and gradually, without sudden changes or revolutions, and only to the extent and in the same proportion as the quantity of money increases or decreases. The relations between the different things and different persons remain the same. If wheat costs a third more, cloth is a third more dear. The landowner who derives five thousand francs from a property worth a hundred thousand francs, derives fifteen thousand francs from the same property when it is worth three hundred thousand francs. And the worker who earns ten pennies a day earns thirty. Every proportion and relation is maintained, and everything is in order, for order is the maintenance of proportions and relations. Those who earn money by their daily work can procure the products of which they daily stand in need; those who can live within the revenue of their capital seek to acquire land, productive land, because the revenue of land is approximately the same as the interest paid for money, and it is more secure because the capital itself is more sheltered from events. Yet when everyone wants to buy, no one wants to sell. Lands are therefore at a high price relative to goods. All the citizens thus aspire to move from being possessors of money to being possessors of land, that is to say to pass from a mobile and dependent political condition to a fixed and independent condition. This is the most happy and most moral cast of the public mind, the one most opposed to the spirit of greed and to revolution. It is what the government should most encourage as the source of many public and private virtues and the most powerful means of the development of all the strengths of society.

---

* EDITOR'S NOTE. The *maximum* was a general price control imposed during the Terror of 1793–1794.

But when money is merchandise, those who have it seek to raise it to the highest price. With money there cannot be a proportion between quantity and need that there is for all others, because it is not really a good, and because the quantity that suffices as a sign does not suffice as merchandise. There are very few sellers and many buyers, so there is not enough competition to lower the price. Goods, therefore, become more expensive, that they might attain, if they can, the price of money; salaries also rise, in order to meet the price of goods, as do taxes. All rise by sudden and disordered shifts, and an irregular and forced progression of all values, a displacement of all the relations upon which ease and fortune repose, spurs on the greedy man and unsettles and torments the moderate one. As the interest, or rather the price of money, is infinitely greater than the produce of the earth, everyone wishes to sell his land in order to procure some money to lend. Instead of purchasing lands with money, he buys money with lands. But when everyone wants to sell, no one wants to buy. The produce of the land or of industry tend to rise to the highest prices, and the lands themselves fall to the lowest, or they are unable to be sold at any price, and one buys only what misery leaves behind or revolutions make available. Everyone aspires to pass from the fixed and independent condition of landowners to the mobile and precarious condition of possessors of money. One notes a general tendency to leave one's home and the home of one's fathers, to leave one's family and country. A vague restlessness and desire for change torments landowners. They complain of being attached to an estate burdened with so many cares, accidents, costs, and surcharges, and with too little income left to pay for their luxuries and pleasures. This cast of mind is most dangerous. It is destructive of every public and private fortune in every State, and especially in an agrarian State.

Those, however, who have had the misfortune to borrow money, or rather to buy it, are constrained to repay it. Landowners abandon their possessions to their creditors. Merchants fail to meet their contracts. Walls are plastered with notices of liquidation and foreclosure sales, and scandals and suffering abound. The sale of lands proceeds only by forced expropriations, and the sale of products proceeds only by bankruptcies. I speak here only of the exterior and commercial effects of the sale of money. What if I were to consider its influence upon the morals of man and the habits of a nation?

Then we would see a devouring, universal greed, which feeds upon a rapid and forced circulation of money, and an inextinguishable thirst for gold, which is esteemed not because it is rare, but because it is dear. We would see an immoderate desire to become rich, extending even to the lowest class of people, and, in some of them, causing horrible disorders and unheard of crimes, while in others, giving rise to a cold, hard egotism, and, in almost everyone, leading to a universal cooling of charity, a total extinction of every generous sentiment, and an insensible transformation of the most disinterested and most friendly nation into a people of stock-jobbers who see in the events of society only chances for gain or loss and in a troop of enemies taking arms against them only public misery and private misfortune.

When Is It Licit to Lend at Interest?

The last question that poses itself is to know under what conditions one may legitimately lend at interest, or, in other words, in what circumstances a profit, even a legal one, becomes legitimate.

In our day, religion and politics have been divided over the question of lending at interest, because religion has taken for the basis of its decisions a concern for public utility, while politics has consulted only the motives of personal interest.

Religion wants to make us all good, politics to make us all rich. Religion, by a happy alchemy, even makes the poor somewhat rich, by the moderation that she imparts to their desires, while the rich she seeks to make poor, by the spirit in which she would have them possess their riches, and by the use that they make of them. She also attempts to prevent a rupture between these two classes, which are always together but are secretly enemies, for this division was the great scandal of pagan society. This she could not prevent even among the rude people whom she called to better laws, by ordaining after a certain length of time the abolition of debts contracted and the return of alienated inheritances. Yet in prescribing work to the domestic man and the most noble cares to the public man, religion, in the Old Law, and even in the New,[4] seems to prefer the cultivation and the possession of the land, given to man as the place of his exile and the subject of his labors. This kind of work preserves the family, and, holding man equally distant from opulence and need, binds man to his fellow by a reciprocity of help and services, and even to his Creator, whose wisdom, power, and goodness are declared by the admirable order of nature. If the doctrines that disfigured the idea of the Divinity began with agricultural peoples, the doctrines that denied the Divinity were born only amidst commercial peoples. Religion does not prohibit the profits of a legitimate commerce. She does, however, fear for her children in that hazardous profession that continually throws the mind of man and his fortune into the opposite extremes of fear and hope, opulence and misery, that can profit from private distress and even from public misfortune, and in which man, strong from his own work alone, needs neither the dew from the sky nor the fat of the land, and seems to await nothing from men, and to have nothing to ask from God.[5] Religion has not disdained to share in the landed property of the nations. She has consecrated to her worship the first fruits of their harvests. The institutions she has founded—institutions protected from need by their common wealth, and from greed by their private poverty—are models for every society. They teach what society's motto should be: *Privatus illis census erat brevis, commune, magnum.*[6] They taught agriculture to the barbarians and cleared the forests and marshes that covered the better part of Europe. Everywhere the cultivation of the land has begun with the worship of God. The Christian religion lifts its sights higher. In her profound politics, which history justifies on every page, she knows that public virtues are the true wealth of States, and that moderation in power, devotion in ministry, obedience in the subject, attachment to political and religious laws, unity among the citizenry, affection for one's land, and the readiness to sacrifice oneself in its defense, are but rarely to be found among a commercial people, who are always agitated by their passions until the day they are subjugated by their neighbors. The Christian religion has wished to make stable societies, not opulent ones.

For a long time our governments have tread other paths. They have not considered wealth as the inevitable and almost unfortunate result of work, but as the goal of all their labors and of all man's industriousness, and the unique end toward which they should hasten by the shortest possible route. They have promoted every means of commerce in order that their wealth might grow, and soon, worn out by their ever-increasing inequality—the necessary result of their commercial successes, they have invented luxury as a means of equalizing fortunes, and they have been able to enrich some only at the cost of corrupting the others. The rich are no longer spenders, they are consumers. The poor are no longer brothers who must be granted their share, but the hungry who must be appeased, or enemies before whom one must capitulate. These base notions, put in the place of moral ideas, have stripped the wealthy of their dignity and the poor of their reserve. The extravagant use of wealth ignited a frenzied greed and gave birth to a criminal speculation. Every desire took up arms and awaited only the signal: It was given, and never have the people seemed more defenseless against their own passions and against those of their neighbors. Everywhere men indifferent to everything other than money have seen revolutions in their countries only as occasions to buy confiscated goods, and war as but the chance to sell provisions, just as they see in famine only wheat to be sold and in an epidemic only inheritances to collect.

We must look to general considerations such as these when we seek the reason for the severity of our religious laws against lending, and for the relaxation of the civil laws. The change in the laws has created a division between a man's interest and his conscience, and a battle ensues in which either fortune suffers or probity succumbs. Timid men ruin themselves by their delicacy; men more free in their morals prey upon the honesty of their neighbor. The union of the citizens, which can be founded only upon common principles and reciprocal esteem, is lost. Some now find pathways to wealth that others will not permit themselves to take. The scandal of differing opinions about moral practice that results is the most grave social disorder imaginable.

I come to the question of lending at interest. There is no difficulty with it when the money is employed in the acquisition of a landed property or another immovable good, such as a house, or some public good which naturally and legitimately brings a revenue, whether the capitalist himself acquires the productive object, or whether lending his money to the acquirer, because in this last case he really buys, under the name of another, and he retains until the reimbursement. The placement of funds in the deposit of an office or the holding as custodian of the rights of an heir whose portion naturally produces a revenue—if it is in land—or a legitimate interest—if it is in money—offer other justifications to the charging of interest.

Nor is there a difficulty with the division of profits or losses in a commercial enterprise. The question is not whether money can produce six per cent when it is employed to make possible a manufacturing interest that produces a profit of fifteen per cent, for in such a case one may even take fifteen per cent for the profit. The question, however, is whether money can return a profit of fifteen per cent when invested in a business that only turns a profit of six per cent, or no profit at all.

Money lent for the acquisition of immovable goods, therefore, legitimately produces interest that should be calculated based on the general and ordinary revenue of the immovable goods. Money invested in a commercial enterprise can legitimately produce a profit that should be calculated with respect to the particular profit of the kind of commerce.

What remains is the simple or daily loan, the loan that, having been contracted for no productive object, offers no public and legal reason for charging interest. Now usury, independent of the rate of interest, is, in the final analysis, interest charged without justification. This is the correct and complete definition of the matter.

The author of an article in the *Publiciste* of September 12, 1806, advanced three arguments for the permission to charge interest for any money lent.

First, "the utility that the lender might derive from the capital if he had not lent it." To this he should have added "if he had used it to acquire productive values or invested it in a commercial venture," for money left in a strong box produces nothing for its possessor. This argument is legitimate; this is the *lucrum cessans* of the theologians. Yet the lender must have had the will and the opportunity to derive a real and legitimate profit from his money, and he must be able to say truthfully to his borrower: "You will pay me interest because I am depriving myself of an assured profit by lending to you."

Second, "the advantage that accrues to the borrower, if someone lends to him."

This argument supposes that the borrower will derive an advantage from the loan, for if it is only an occasion of loss to him, the argument fails. It would be absurd and inhumane to say to a borrower, ruined by the use to which he had put your money: "Pay me the interest on my money on account of the advantage that you have derived from it." This argument is, in fact, no better than sophistry. It is not the advantage the borrower derives from the money that justifies the interest I charge him, at least as long as I do not agree to share the losses that he might make with that same money. The justification for charging interest is only the loss that he causes me, *damnum emergens,* in depriving me of money that I could have made to bear fruit in some other manner. In fact, in the ordinary course of things, charity does not oblige me to inconvenience myself in order to cause pleasure to my fellow man. Yet it does oblige me to render him all the services I can, and especially not to see with an envious eye the advantages that I can procure for him when no damage to myself results. Here we must distinguish charity from utility, and the service that one renders from the help that one gives. If my carriage overturns on the road, and if laborers paid an hourly wage help me to set it back up, the money that I give to them is the price, not of the service that they have rendered me—for charity is not to be paid for—but of the time that they have spent in coming to my assistance, and that they could have employed in other work. This is so true that if men of a more elevated rank came to my assistance, I would offend them by offering money to them because themselves not being able to charge the price of the time that they would have employed in manual and lucrative work, they could not consider the money that I offered them as anything other than a payment for the charity that they had shown to me. Thus it is the loss that the lender suffers, and not the advantage derived by the borrower, that justifies the interest charged by the lender.

Third, "an insurance against the dangers of late payment and possible loss." "This insurance," the author continues, "should be made with respect to the prevailing political circumstances and civil laws, as well as the nature of the borrower's affairs, his moral character, and his ability to deceive the lender."

This argument demands a lengthy discussion, for if, as the author I cite expressly states, beggars should not be treated as lords upon the earth, neither should usurers be the only judges of their own affairs.

What I would say to the lender is this: "In the interest you would charge you seek an insurance against the danger of late payment and the reimbursement of possible losses. I understand you. You regard the loan as a contract in which both parties agree to compensate the other for possible damages. Very well, but note that the insurance is only for you, and far from guaranteeing your borrower against any loss, the interest that you charge him adds to his losses in the case of misfortune. Even in calculating the insurance that you demand for political events, civil laws, the possibility of deceit, and the borrower's moral character—all vague, arbitrary, and uncertain things that imagination and greed can inflate or minimize at whim—you would make your borrower pay for hypothetical dangers while you yourself do not take into account the most ordinary setbacks that he might suffer. In the most common contract of this sort, that of maritime insurance, the chance of risk is presumed. It is even foreseen by law, which does not permit you to derive a profit from the success without agreeing to shoulder your portion of the loss. Moreover, if the insured cargo is lost, the law, which obliges you to pay the insurance, gives you no further recourse against the pirate who captured the boat than against the sea that swallowed it up or the fire that consumed it. In a loan, on the contrary, you may, it is true, fear a loss, as one vaguely fears every possible evil. But you may not presume it, for then you would surely not lend your money. Nor does the law presume it, insofar as it gives you every means to prevent it and to repair it. It accords you, in case of late payment, the interest of a loan from the day on which you may rightly demand the return of the capital. You may consign your debtor to prison, or seize and sell his possessions until you are paid what you are owed. You have paid yourself for the danger of loss and have made loss impossible for you either by taking as security property of greater value than the money you lent, or by lending for such a short term that your lender will not have the time to fail to meet his payments, or by requiring one or more signatures of persons known to be solvent, or by consenting to a double title, which in truth exposes the heirs of the borrower to pay twice, or your heirs to exact, double the original sum. You have insured your capital, not only against the danger of a possible bankruptcy, but even against the misfortune of an actual bankruptcy. You have therefore paid yourself in advance for losses that may never come and which, thanks to your precautions, cannot come."

It is, moreover, the shareholders who lose in the misfortunes of commerce and never those who have lent large sums. Only a disaster like an avalanche in Switzerland that wipes out whole villages, with their tools and their land, can frustrate the precautions of the merchants of money.

Thus in the case of the loan, the real profit of which one is deprived, or the actual damage that one suffers, are justifications for charging interest. But supposed profits or damages, or insurance against imaginary damages, or the need of the lender or the borrower, are not justifications, as long as the condition of a society in political and commercial revolution does not render every fortune mobile, every property uncertain, ever danger imminent, and, consequently, every precaution licit and every means of reimbursement legitimate. But whether this ever be the case, I will not be so bold as to say.

Here we must lift our minds to more general considerations, and as students of politics consider how the nature of transactions is altered by the charging of interest on loans.

In the past, the different classes of citizens possessed different kinds of properties, corresponding to the diversity of their duties and functions in society. The families and the corporate bodies devoted to public service possessed rents in land or landed properties, considerable enough to be cared for by tenant farmers or sharecroppers and almost always inalienable. The bourgeois, whether lawyers or businessmen, possessed rents constituted in money. The inhabitants of the countryside, whether farmhands or yeomen, cultivated their heritage with their hands. This distribution of property favored public order: It left the leading classes of society entirely free for public service in the Church, on the bench, or in the army. The people—who can never be sufficiently protected from idleness or from a tendency to vagrancy—it attached to the land. The bourgeois it allowed to devote themselves without distraction to the study of the law or the pursuit of their affairs.

This arrangement was favorable to the domestic economy and the permanence of communities and families. It preserved the fortunes of public men during their separation from the land and from the paucity of attention that they were able to give to their property. It tended to increase the ease of the laborer, and rendered the condition of the capitalist almost as fixed as that of the landowner. The dying father of a family who left to his children capital placed in a fixed investment did not fear that this would become an occasion of prodigality or of risky speculation and ruin. These permanent investments, with their annual revenues and their thirty-year terms, were able to fix families in the places where they were established and prevented those senseless emigrations that depopulate a land of its ancient inhabitants and break the hereditary bonds of family relation and friendship between the citizens of the same region, and sooner or later lead to the ruin of families. I do not fear to say it: If a few fortunes have been made thanks to the availability of capital for short-term loans, a very large number of families have been dissolved and have lost their possessions by this same mobility, which has placed the fruits of the savings and work of several generations in the hands of the dissolute and senseless and at the mercy of perilous endeavors. It was, however, through these permanent placements of capital, so denigrated today, that so many modest fortunes were honestly and slowly built up and preserved through domestic and public crises, fortunes the modesty of which was more favorable to good morals and was equally distant from the scandalous opulence and the unruly misery that are the sad fruits of the speculation that has succeeded them.

The system of John Law,* philosophico-economical theories about the nature of money and its circulation, fraudulent dealings with landed rents, loans that terminate with the life of a person, lotteries, and games of chance: All these incitements to greed, all these appeals to egotism, which in society see only the individual and in time only the present moment, have set in motion every desire, every hope, every principle, and every fortune. The landowner has sold his lands to place them in rents; the capitalist has converted his long-term leases to short-term ones; the craftsman has wagered his children's bread in the lotteries; and all of them, greedy for pleasures, and for immediate and selfish pleasures, have consumed a useless life in the isolation of a criminal celibacy, or remorselessly cast off to the following generation the burden of their needs and the task of rebuilding their fortune. Luxury, once unknown in the provinces and more restrained in the capital, and the variations of fashion, ridiculous because ever-changing and culpable because costly, have replaced our fathers' frugality and noble simplicity. The most shocking extremes are born of the exaggeration

---

* EDITOR'S NOTE: John Law (1671–1729), a Scottish financier, was comptroller general of France during the Regency (1715–1723), during which he presided over a failed scheme for the use of paper money.

of every means of amassing wealth and spending it. There is more extravagance and more suffering, more superfluity and more real need, more pleasure and less charity, more commerce and less good faith, more movement and less order, more private interest and less public affection.

Long-term placements of capital, favorable to public order and to the domestic economy, also assist agricultural and commercial enterprises much more than do short-term ones. Upon a sum of capital that he keeps longer and at a lower rate of interest, the borrower can build more assured hopes of making or repairing his fortune. Today the farmer cannot and should not dare to be a borrower; and the merchant, who still runs that ruinous chance, obtaining money only at great cost and for a very short term, risks hurrying his affairs in order more quickly to dispense himself from the heavy burden of interest payments. He tries the most perilous paths and sometimes the least honest ones, because they are the most expeditious. Ceaselessly looking to find money today with which to pay tomorrow's debt, uncertain in the morning whether he will be dishonored by evening, his time is consumed with his changing balance sheet and his business with contracting or repaying loans: A deplorable condition that weakens, and even kills commerce, and which, joined to the luxury that has been in our time introduced into that modest and moderate class to the point where it regards itself as the first and the most useful, leads, sooner or later, to those scandalous bankruptcies in which public opinion does not distinguish between the unfortunate gentleman and the impudent cheat, and with which those who lend for short terms and at high rates of interest are the accomplices rather than the victims.

Thus the judges, when consulted upon article 71 of the proposed Civil Code—which reads "the rate of interest in commerce is regulated like the sale of merchandise"—attempted to demonstrate the fatal consequences to commerce of an excessive and arbitrary rate of interest, and have unanimously demanded the rejection of a law that would declare money to be merchandise. The tribunal of Reims, placed amidst a land both commercial and agrarian, has gone further, and has spoken in these terms: "When confidence in commerce is well-established, and when good morals presided over his transactions, the honest merchant and the industrious manufacturer found sure resources well-proportioned to his needs in the long-term contracts of which the annual interest—fixed and regulated by law—was always proportionate to the productivity of industry. The reimbursement, left to the will of the borrower, gave him the necessary time to make the investment profit, to increase or to consolidate his fortune, until the time when, having become master of his affairs, he believed himself to be able to disengage his possessions from liens by retiring the loans. But it is very different today: the merchant finds himself at the mercy of speculators, and he succumbs, forced as he is to submit to their laws."

I will finish what I have to say about long-term placements of capital with two important reflections.

The first is that long-term placements of capital were entirely according to the spirit of a monarchical constitution of society, in which everything, even fortunes, tends to fixity, to permanence, and to moderation, while loans for short terms and without justification, introduced in Europe since the Reformation, are very much in accord with the spirit of popular government, in which everything tends toward mobility, change, and an exaggerated use of all things, and where everything is short-term: order, repose, fortunes, life, customs, laws, and society itself.

It is, therefore, only since European society has been poised on the edge of the abyss of democracy that short-term lending, more universally practiced, and a rapid circulation of money, have made long-term placements of capital fall into disuse, and even, in the end, have rendered odious long-term leases of the land, the most free, most useful, most moral, and surely the most political of all contracts.

My other reflection is that capital placed in long-term contracts being, like capital placed in landed property, alienated for an indefinite time—the term of which was according to the will of the borrower alone—it was reasonable to suppose that the borrower, as long as he kept the sum, would derive some advantage from it, and that the lender, while he was deprived of it, would suffer some damage, because it was probable that if it had been at his disposal, he would have put it to useful employment in one way or another. In such a case, the advantage of the borrower joined the damages that the lender might have suffered to justify the charging of interest.

Be that as it may, it is not impossible to reestablish the practice of long-term placements of capital and to constitute lending at interest as we have constituted so many other things. It is even likely that we will return to it, and perhaps with modifications that will render the condition of the two parties more equal.

It would be useful at this point to recall the series of questions that we proposed at the outset of our discussion.

Money neither has value nor is merchandise, but it is the public sign of all values, and the legal means of exchange among all kinds of merchandise.

Money legitimately yields interest when it is employed to acquire something that naturally or legitimately produces a revenue.

Money legitimately yields dividends when it is employed in a commercial enterprise.

Interest should be fixed at the rate of the presumed revenue of landed property, the source of all productivity and the regulator of all values.

Dividends should vary with the profits of commerce.

Money can yield interest when the lender renounces a guaranteed profit, or when he suffers a real damage, as in the loan from one merchant to another, and in this case the interest can even be the just equivalent of the profit that he loses or the damage that he suffers.

A long-term placement of capital legitimately yields a profit because it is impossible that at one time or another the lender might not have derived a profit from the money that he has alienated from himself for an indefinite length of time.

Short-term lending, however, which does not involve either the acquisition of something productive or a common commercial enterprise, and in which the lender, disposing his capital at all times, cannot allege either a profit that he must renounce or a damage that he might suffer, does not legitimately produce interest. Such loans have until recently been considered as loans for consumption, and essentially interest-free. The reason for this is plain. In fact, because money is only the sign of productive or unproductive values, short-term loans not made for the sake of acquiring something productive cannot be other than the sign of unproductive values in goods or in services. But if one hundred francs loaned for a short term are the sign of ten measures of wheat or fifty days of work, by what right would I require the borrower to repay me eleven measures of wheat or fifty-five days of work?

Insurance against the danger of a possible loss is not a sufficient justification for charging interest because this insurance is provided by the precautions that the law allows the lender to take in order to prevent his loss.

The service rendered to the borrower is not a sufficient justification, because this service, which I render to him without inconveniencing myself, is a charity that I owe to my brother, and that he owes me in his turn, and which can neither be measured in terms of money nor bought.

I recall here the laws that were formerly in use in France and their justification. Our society prospered under the protection of these laws, and by them our conduct was raised to the highest point of decency and dignity. I will not hide the truth: These laws were severe, as are all laws whose object is to subordinate private interest to public. The prohibition of short-term lending doubtless posed obstacles to the affairs of a family; but the toleration of these loans produces an intolerable disorder in the affairs of the State. In vain is it said that the law that prohibited them would not be obeyed. I would respond that if the administration must sometimes prevent what it cannot outlaw, morals must always outlaw even what cannot be entirely prevented.

We have discovered the reason for our religious laws about lending, although we sought only the justification for our political laws. This is a new proof for the truth of Christian doctrine: the perfect conformity on all objects of morals with the most natural condition of things. Those who stubbornly oppose the Church may remark that I have treated the question of lending politically and not as a theologian: But it is not my fault if true philosophy entirely accords with religion.

Long treatises have been written about the wealth of nations, treatises teaching with great erudition what everyone already knows, and sometimes even what no one could ever know. I doubt that there exist works that are more abstract, or more useless. Yet, in the end, do the words "the wealth of nations" present an idea distinct enough to be the subject of a treatise, or even the title of a work? Private individuals are wealthy, and nations are strong. As opulence makes the political force of a private individual, one may say that strength is the only wealth of a nation. One must therefore treat of the wealth of private individuals and the strength of nations: But is it necessary to devote oneself to a laborious search for the nature and cause of wealth? Do not the children of this world, as the Gospel tells us, already know more than the children of light about the means of getting wealth? Is not the art of making oneself rich already more well-known to the ignorant than to the wise and to men of spirit? To consider wealth in nations: Does not extreme misery go hand in hand with extreme opulence? Is not the nation with the most millionaires always the one that contains the most paupers? Morton Eden's *The State of the Poor** ought to be read, for there one will read of towns, even large ones, in which half the inhabitants are under the care of the bureau of charity. Every people that is content with its sort is always wealthy enough; and, in this regard, barren Sweden was as wealthy as florid Holland, and it was much stronger. The wealth of a nation is not the taxes it pays, for taxes are needs and not a product; and the excess of needs is rather a sign of distress than the measure of wealth. I repeat: The wealth of a nation is its strength, and its strength is in its constitution, its morals, and its laws, and not in its money. One can even be certain that given equal territory and population, the more opulent nation, that is to say the more commercial one, will be the weaker, because it will be the more corrupt, and that with the worst of all corruptions, the corruption of greed.

Let it be said today, not to blame the past, but to teach the future: It is less political fanaticism than the universal greed produced by the new systems of money, and by the relaxation of all the principles of morals, that has caused Christian society, once among the most generous and most enlightened of peoples, to descend below even those ignoble and delirious pagan demagogic regimes, which levied judgment upon bare accusations, governed by punishment, lived by theft, and in which exile and death were the inevitable reward for a life of virtue.

We believe ourselves to be wealthy, and we are, but with artificial goods. Yet true goods are being exhausted, and nature seems to be becoming impoverished. There are few towns in France in which it is not easier to purchase a piece of mahogany furniture than an oak beam to hold up the roof of one's house. Wood to burn costs almost as much as the food that one prepares with it; and cloth from India may be had at a better price than fabric made of the wool from our flocks. How can it be that our modern

---

* EDITOR'S NOTE: Sir Frederick Morton Eden's *The State of the Poor: A History of the Labouring Classes in England, with Parochial Reports* (London, 1797) was published in a French translation in 1800.

inventions lead at the same time to the enjoyment of the most refined luxuries and the dearness of our primary needs?

We can clean our laundry by gas, light our apartments with gas, heat ourselves with steam, and the like. Machines are replacing men, and even the elements, if we are to believe Condorcet, will one day convert themselves into substances fitting for our nourishment. Everywhere we are prodigal with art in order to economize with nature. I applaud these discoveries, and I admire their authors; but perhaps we should bemoan the cause that renders these discoveries necessary and men so inventive. To the extent that luxury wins over society, will we lack our primary necessities? Will the first gifts of nature, that Providence has scattered abroad with so liberal a hand to all her children, and with which young nations are so abundantly provided, begin to be exhausted in an advanced society, when we, as wastrels, after having consumed our own patrimony, are reduced to seeking our livelihood from the precarious means of industry? Will we, alas!, then need to be taught the learned equations of chemistry or the ingenious inventions of mechanics in order to practice the once-simple art of living? Will our physical life become as troublesome as our political life? This I know not. But our large cities in Europe already resemble places besieged for several years, in which, after the stores have been exhausted, recourse is made to less natural means. We heat our rooms by burning our furniture, make money out of paper, eat whatever is at hand, and by these our privations prolong the dolorous existence of an exhausted garrison. |•

Notes

[1] Statesmen they were not, those writers of the last century who placed the cultivation of grain above the pasturing of livestock, wrongly recommending both the exhaustion of the soil and the division of the commons, the most deadly of all their works. The pasturing of livestock, which is productive for a longer time and with more certainty, preserves the primitive youthfulness of the land, and maintains its beauty, its verdure, and its trees. The culture of the fields wears out the land and spoils it. Man the shepherd and hunter, consequently, is more sober, more healthy, more robust, more agile, less attached to

the land, less greedy, and readier to serve the needs of society. Given equal means, a nation of shepherds will defeat a nation of planters. Happy the people who, in an advanced age, retain something of the first habits of society! Today we are rediscovering these truths. The government encourages the raising of flocks and the cultivation of artificial prairies. Yet the shrinking of the forests, in certain provinces, is disturbing. Commerce and luxury consume them and have not been able to reproduce them. Coal from the earth will supply the defect in some places, but this fuel, be it as healthy as wood, blackens everything, spreads a disagreeable odor, depresses man, and may, given time, alter the nation's temperament.

2 "Men are born and live equal in their rights" is an abstract proposition that applies to nothing; "power is essentially good" is a proposition whose moral truth, independent of the individual who exercises the power, applies to every society.

3 Someone asked Cato: *Quid est fenerare?* (What is lending at interest?) He replied: *Quid est occidere?* (What is murder?)

4 Jesus Christ, in the Gospels, takes almost all of his comparisons from the landowning family and the cultivation of the earth.

5 It is, I believe, to this cause that should be attributed the frequent suicides of our commercial cities. The man who can attribute his success only to himself has no one else to blame for his failures, and he punishes himself for his faults. The farmer supports his losses without despairing because he sees in them a cause superior to his own abilities. I do not believe that suicides are to be found in the countryside, even among those poor wretches who escaped from the horrible disaster that struck Switzerland, in which families, belongings, and homes disappeared in an instant.

6 Private things they held cheap, but common things dear.

3 | 1810
On the Wealth
of Nations

ADAM SMITH has written at length about the *Nature and the Causes of the Wealth of Nations.* I open his book, and I see that it concerns the produce of the soil and of industry, commerce, the mechanical arts, manufactures, the distribution of work, the apportioning of shares, the accumulations of capital, interest paid for loans, salaries, and the like. That is to say, it is a treatise of the wealth of individuals who are landowners, merchants, capitalists, bankers, laborers, manufacturers, artisans, and so on, and not of the *Wealth of Nations*, which is not and cannot be any of these things.

Some might say that because a nation is a collection of individuals, the national wealth consists in the sum of the wealth of individuals. Yet this principle may be contested. One may instead defend the view that a nation is, as a society, something greater than a collection of individuals. Moreover, to be able to call the sum of the wealth of individuals the wealth of the nation, it would have to be the case that every individual participated in this wealth, for the nation is composed of every individual without exception, and wealth is not something abstract. It is difficult to conceive of a nation that could be rich while a considerable portion of its children suffers from extreme want. This is, however, the case, and, throughout Europe, there are nowhere more paupers than in those nations called wealthy. In Switzerland, as Malthus notes in his excellent *Essay on the Principle of Population*, the largest numbers of beggars are found near the wealthiest towns.

If one is to consider the wealth of individuals as forming the wealth of nations, there will not be, strictly speaking, either poor or rich nations, because in the rich nations there are always many poor individuals, and in the poorest nations many wealthy ones.

It must be noted that I am here considering only civilized nations. These are the only ones that can be compared with one another, because in them wealth is composed of the same elements, and the right to property reposes upon the same laws.

Wealth, taken in a general and philosophical sense, is the means of existence and conservation; and *opes*, in the Latin tongue, signifies both wealth and strength.

For the individual—a physical being—these means are material wealth, the produce of soil and of industry, or the sign that represents all these goods and serves to procure them.

For society—a moral being—the means of existence and duration are moral riches, and the forces of conservation are, for the domestic society, morals, and for the public society, laws. Yes, society is a moral body: Religion is its health, the monarchy, its strength, and the virtues its possessions. War, disease, and famine cannot destroy it, yet a book suffices to cause a revolution.

Morals and laws are, therefore, the true and even the only wealth of societies, families, and nations. That is to say, they are the true and the only means of their existence and conservation. They are even the only wealth that it is suitable to discuss. Nations should only be instructed in the virtues. Nor do individuals need to be told about wealth, because for the common run of men, personal interest—that most enlightened of all masters—teaches them enough to busy themselves fruitfully with material wealth and the means of reproducing and conserving it. I even believe that under this heading the work of Adam Smith teaches only what has been known by all peoples and practiced by the majority of individuals since the very origin of nations. Wealth is the natural consequence of work, and if men are to be made rich, it suffices to keep them busy, without plaguing them with talk about wealth.

The force of nations, even their moral force alone, which comes from their constitution and their political and religious laws, is thus their true wealth. As to physical force, which comes from the population and its means of subsistence, it exists necessarily in more or less every nation, as there can be no nation without a sufficient population, nor a population without the means of subsistence. It is the moral force of which Tacitus spoke when he contrasted the vigor of the Germans' morals to the opulence and luxury of the

Parthians. And this is what we find expressed poetically in the Book where everything is to be found. The Psalmist tells us that the foreigners, to whom justice means only strength, have said: "Our children grow in their youth like new plants; our daughters rise up like the columns of a temple; our cellars and granaries pour forth all manner of fruits; our flocks are fertile and our cattle always fat: happy the people that has all these good things! And we say: 'Happy the people that has God for its Lord!'" That nation is happy, that is, whose laws are in conformity with the relations that the supreme legislator has established among men for the conservation of societies.

It might be said that a nation has wealth in its public property, in its possessions dedicated to some public service, such as the temples of religion and of justice, asylums for the poor, houses of public education, and the like. Yet besides the fact that Smith has hardly spoken of this kind of wealth in treating the *Wealth of Nations*, it is easy to see that these public properties form a part of, even a direct part of, the moral force that a constitution and its laws give to a people, because public properties—which all nations have according to their needs—are the necessary means of executing the constitution and its laws.

Nor are taxes themselves a kind of wealth; they are a need. And greater needs are not the same as greater wealth.

Moral force is, therefore, I repeat, the true wealth of a nation, and the unique means of its conservation. In fact, an independent nation ceases to endure because of the viciousness of its laws rather than because of a defect in population, territory, or industrial wealth, for a vicious constitution prevents it from making good use of its population and of the produce of its soil and industry—either for internal or external defense—and even sometimes turns to its loss all its natural or acquired means of defense. It is certainly not for want of men and money that Turkey has fallen progressively into the final stages of political weakness. And Poland—the only State to have gained its independence since the days of Charlemagne that has been erased from the list of Christian nations—certainly had a sufficient population and the means of subsistence necessary to endure, if it had also some principle of conservation in its constitution, or, rather, if its constitution, contrary to the nature of society as it was, had not contained the seeds that sooner or later had to lead the country to destruction, even if it had not had any neighbors.

A family also conserves itself by its morals rather than by its wealth; and when its morals are corrupted—that is, when the natural relations among the persons who compose it are misunderstood—then great wealth is, just as is extreme want, a cause of decadence, because it offers more encouragement and opportunity to the passions.

Adam Smith has therefore not treated the *Wealth of Nations*. It is more important than one might think to note the error in his title because it has had the greatest influence upon public opinion and administrative measures in the various States of Europe, whose governments have accustomed themselves to regarding money and all that reproduces it—in a word, wealth, material wealth—as the unique source of the strength of nations, and have made all of their decisions with the object of acquiring it.

In the end, every nation—like every family—that subsists from the produce of its soil and its industry is as wealthy as any other, even if it has less money. If a nation or a family cannot subsist from its produce, it will perish, that is to say that the nation will fall into a real dependence upon a neighboring nation and become a province, and the family, according to the prevailing form of government, will be reduced to a state of domestic service or slavery. The price in money of those things necessary for life indicates both the state of the population and the quantity of the means of subsistence. Setting aside other considerations, these are at a low price when the population is weak and at a very high price wherever the population is excessive, because the large number of the consumers makes the means of subsistence dear. This last condition, if it be general and prolonged for some time, menaces a State with trouble and individuals with suffering; and then a nation is truly poor, even amidst an abundance of coinage.

In order to observe the changes that have taken place in the general spirit of European governments relative to political economy and their opinion about the wealth of nations, we must consider the matter again from a higher vantage point.

Christian Europe, which might be considered the Estates-General of the civilized world, was composed of different orders of nations, just as the Estates-General of a particular society is composed of different orders of citizens.

There were nations that may have been called noble. They were landowners of a large property, among whom sentiments were elevated, characters generous, and habits martial. They made war to exercise their strength and to uphold their dignity rather than to enlarge their possessions. The most powerful among them owed their growth more to the authority of their laws than to the force of their arms.

Some nations were mercantile, others manufacturing, some purely agricultural, and some even simply transported goods: These may be called the Third Estate of nations. They were rich in their capital and industry, and exclusively occupied with the care of making them grow by every sort of means.

This is not to say that in all of these nations there were not individuals who were nobles, merchants, artisans, members of the clergy, and so forth. I wish only to speak of the dominant spirit in each nation, the most constant habits of individuals, and of the profession which, considered in general, held the first rank in them and was, as it were, the pivot on which their politics turned.

In the time of which I speak, and which is already separated from us by several centuries, the leading nations—France, Spain, Germany, and Poland—were little concerned to know whether what has since been called the balance of trade was in their favor—whether their manufactures were all that was required for their needs or luxuries, and whether the secondary nations were victorious over them by importing or exporting on their own vessels either the foreign or indigenous produce of soil or industry. They were somewhat like great lords who saw it as part of their function to support in their service a crowd of workers of all kinds, and who, occupied with the important cares of public society, relied upon mercenaries for the direction of their domestic affairs, and did not think to profit from their tradesmen or tenant farmers by employing their men or horses to transport to the market the goods that crossed their lands, or to go seek the objects necessary for the consumption of their households. There was doubtless less money in circulation; but there was less greed as well, because nature, which watches over our virtues as over our subsistence, does not permit us to keep her products for long, and avarice can lock away in its coffers only the sign that represents them. There was less activity among men, but there was less agitation and restlessness in society. There were, finally, fewer events in public society, but I believe, upon strong evidence, that there was more happiness, ease, and even virtue in the family. Their history shone less brilliantly, but their life was more contented.

New ideas spread in Europe toward the beginning of the fifteenth century, and in the general politics of the civilized world, and in the particular politics of each State, a revolution was insensibly accomplished that was closely similar, in its principle and its effects, to the French Revolution, and which was not without its effect upon this last event. All of the great States blushed, as our first parents had done, about a nudity which they had not suspected during their age of innocence, and they hurried to cover themselves. They were all at once possessed with a fury for commerce and by the lust for gold and wished each to have their part of the wealth of the recently discovered New World, cost them what it may. And so was naturally established among all these States, great either by territory or by commerce, a system of equality that was decorated with the name balance of power and in which the voices were counted, as it were, by head rather than by order.

England, till then a power of the second rank, would hold the first place in this new system because of its location and its habits. Here France, which had never before had the commercial spirit, lost her relative superiority. Later, under the most power of monarchs, she was even reduced to enduring the haughtiness of Holland, that upstart, proud of her opulence and of the rank she had usurped.

Administration, even in France, passed into the hands of a second order of citizens who brought to it their cast of mind and habits. There was no longer any interest except in manufacturing, commerce, and the circulation of money. They soon invented banks, State bonds, loans, and lotteries. The governments even made bankrupts. Bankruptcy became almost a badge of honor, and, in some sense, the means of legitimizing oneself in the political world as a man of commerce. Politics, with eyes constantly fixed upon the balance of trade and the balance of power, became the attempt to make the continual oscillations pay in one's favor and thus to find repose amidst perpetual movement. The science of administration became more complicated, without for that being more trustworthy or more enlightened. One spoke of the public credit, and the strength of

States, like government bonds, became something to be wagered upon; and all these balances, all these proportions, and all these games of chance, produced only swaying and fluctuations in the States, took away every fixed foundation from society, and all security from private fortunes, and sapped the foundations of public and private morals.

When the States that I have called noble became commercial, that is to say much occupied with the commerce of private individuals, it was proposed, as a necessary consequence, that their noblemen become merchants. Upon this subject, books and even laws were written in order to permit the nobility to trade without derogation of dignity or duties. Fortunately, our morals rejected these laws, and, as almost always happens in innovations that have to do with morals, the people—whose natural good sense was not tricked by these specious systems—showed itself to be more sensible than the government. Commerce is always being spoken of as the universal bond of peoples, yet never has there been a more active cause of bloodier or more intractable wars. The constant goal of governments was to isolate some States from the others, by combining systems of reciprocal prohibitions, and especially by seeking to domesticate the produce of soil or industry that was growing or was being manufactured in the other.

It was then natural that one often spoke of national wealth, and that one placed in money and commerce the means of force and conservation that our fathers saw only in religion, the monarchy, and public spirit, and which alone had, for so many centuries and through all sorts of political crises, led the continental nations, each in its turn, to glory and empire.

The religious and political laws that had hitherto governed the States of Europe and formed the public spirit appeared not to favor commerce and the rapid circulation of money. If the letter still remained, the spirit fell into disuse, and the force of conservation was weakened in every State. There was not, nor could there have been, a public spirit, nor even energy, maintained in a commercial and manufacturing nation devoted to calculations of personal interest, and still less today when the laws of war protect the personal property of the vanquished and in our humanitarian sentiments we call it a crime for a citizen not to be paid to defend his land.

Lord Feldkirk, after having spoken of the martial spirit, the generous habits, and the exalted and romantic character of the Scottish highlanders, complained of their wont to emigrate to America since the changes that had came over their land after the battle of Culloden: "If there is some means of retaining these men in their homes, it can only be the introduction of some new branch of industry. If we were to succeed in this, these men would take on the way of life and the habits of factory workers. They might, as have others, furnish a few recruits, but they would no longer resemble their ancestors." England is the most powerful and even the most warlike of the commercial nations; and yet, in spite of what is said of their public spirit—which has never been put to the ultimate test, and which is at bottom only a spirit of defiance toward its own government and a jealousy of other nations—there is not a sensible man in Europe, nor perhaps in England, who thinks that the English people can find in its public spirit and its energy the means to repel an invasion.

Whenever this commercial spirit and these new means of work and of wealth were introduced, they caused the fields of agriculture to be deserted for the cash registers of commerce, the countryside for the cities. The cities grew, populated themselves, and were built up at the expense of the countryside; and the greatest interests of States and the first goods of man—public spirit, morals, and health—did not profit by the exchange.

These are not the worn-out maxims of a stoic philosophy about the disdain for riches; these are the lessons of history, and political truths confirmed by experience. In every era, poor nations have conquered rich ones, even when they held in their wealth and in the ancient right of war the most powerful motives for self-defense, and when the victory would place at the disposition of the victor the vanquished and all that he possessed: "Goods, women, children, temples, even tombs," as Montesquieu said. The prodigious successes of the revolutionary arms of France do not at all contradict this great truth because it was the poorest part of the French nation that was seized by the fanaticism of liberty and equality and descended upon the neighboring nations, and these armies were stripped of all the pomp and luxury that the armies of the European powers carried in their train.

I know that governments no longer believe that they need spirit and energy in the mass of the nation since they have exclusively confided their defense to paid soldiers. We see in history, however, that the people have always raised more determined resistance than have soldiers, and, as may be seen in the history of our own time, that armies have, in general, been strong in the attack but weak in defense.

To counsel a nation to seek the wealth that manufacturing and commerce can procure is to exhort it to renounce all public spirit, all lofty sentiment, all generosity, all disinterestedness, and to wish to discard that noble disdain for wealth that has always characterized great men and great nations in order to throw it into a restless activity whose single motive and sole end is money. This is to make life a torment much more than something to enjoy, for it is to take from us our first and most precious wealth, and life's most powerful means of strength and preservation. How common it is to think incorrectly about this matter. A people indifferent to riches is often considered to be indolent, and it has been forgotten that a nation has more public spirit when its people are less concerned with personal interest.

The wealth of individuals is, therefore, not the wealth of nations, if by wealth one understands the means of existence and of the conservation of society. Far from the opulence of individuals making the strength of a nation, we may, on the contrary, affirm that there is no weaker nation than the one in which every citizen is rich.

Yet if one were to insist upon considering the wealth of individuals as forming the wealth of a nation, it must at least be the case that all the individuals participate in this wealth, as all of them, without exception, contribute to forming the body of the nation. If the rigid partisans of pure democracy think, as follows from their principles, that the general will ceases to exist when one citizen is deprived of the right of manifesting his particular will, it is even more true that one could not speak of national wealth where a numerous part of the nation is in a state of extreme poverty. Nowhere are there more poor or needy people than in the nations made opulent by commerce and manufacturing, which almost always raise the population far above the subsistence that the soil can furnish. England, the richest nation, or at least the one with the most money and the highest wages, can serve as an example for us. Half of the citizens there are at the charge of the other half. The poor tax has become the most onerous of taxes, even for the rich; and we see, by writings recently published in England on this subject, that for a long time the nation has sought the means of ridding itself of a burden that it can no longer support.

We will find another example of this, and a still more decisive one, in one of the small Swiss cantons famous in all times for the well-being of its inhabitants. This is taken from a discourse pronounced by the *Land amman* Hehr of the canton of Glarus to the chamber of commerce of that city: "When the art of working with cotton was brought into this valley, the availability of work and the high price of labor did not fail to attract workers. A spinning-wheel was a dowry; a weaver was a man of ease; men were in a hurry to lend themselves to this kind of work. They enjoyed the present without worrying about the future. And what has happened to this wealth? One quarter of our population receives or begs alms. Upstanding fathers of families, their wives, and their children fight at great cost against misery and hunger; they endure their lot with fortitude, but live amidst anguish and suffering. New habits have led to new needs. The sweet labors of our ancestors have become foreign to us. The sedentary life, an unhealthy diet, and too much time spent in humid and unhealthy places have stripped our people of their health and natural vigor. It pains me to dwell on this spectacle, but I must call your attention to the immediate consequences of our predicament. I must testify to the growth of the population, to the need to support oneself, to the easier congress of persons of different sexes, to the ease of living temporarily provided by industrial work, and to those precocious marriages contracted by children who still have the greatest need for paternal surveillance."

Seize, therefore, every means by which foreign trade may be made to prosper in a land, cover it with workshops, factories, manufactures, render the circulation of money more active, and at all costs force the population to grow beyond the subsistence that the soil can produce or that trade can import, and you may count it as certain that you will soon shut up a part of that artificial population in prisons, poor houses, hospitals, and even in the cemeteries, and subject the other half to rationing. The natural order is thus inverted. Man should find his subsistence in the family that gives birth to him, and when he seeks it from the State—which neither labors nor spins—the government can only give him one by taking away from others, nourish indigent families by impoverishing landowning families, and aid the poor by making others ill-at-ease. Private charity then becomes a subsidy, and public beneficence resembles oppression. When there was neither commerce nor money in European society, the generous dreamt of putting a chicken in every pot. Today, when nations vomit forth money, and cover the seas with their buildings and the markets with their goods, philanthropy, obliged to live from industry, puts them in the economic soup. |•

4 | 1815
A Proposal to Abolish Divorce

Gentlemen,

Y OU HAVE enacted severe laws to provide for the tranquillity of the State. Today we must enact strong laws to assure the stability of the family.

In the primitive and regular order of society, the family becomes the State, and customs become laws. Yet when the State turned against the natural development of society, it gave laws to the family, and these ruled over its way of life, or, rather, abandoned it to lawlessness. Allow me briefly to trace the history of the family, that we might see the birth and the progress of the disorders that have altered its primitive constitution.

Domestic society began with monogamy and the indissolubility of the conjugal bond. The birth of the two sexes in approximately equal numbers is enough to indicate that polygamy does not accord with the plan of nature. Neither could the dissolubility of the conjugal bond, which establishes so cruel an inequality between the two sexes, have entered into the designs of its author. And so the supreme legislator of societies, speaking of the dissolution of marriage, himself says "that it was not thus at the beginning."

As families multiply, they form nations, and all too often unfriendly nations. The dangers of war or the labors of agriculture, endured almost exclusively by one of the two sexes, disturbs their proportion; and, in those fledgling tribes whose first concern is procreation polygamy—which favors procreation in a young nation just as it brings its decline in an advanced nation—introduced itself with the help of those licentious religions that offered up modesty as a sacrifice to their divinities and consecrated prostitution.

The Jewish nation, raised amidst these dangerous examples, and itself too small for the land it had to conquer and for the high destiny to which it was called, could not be held to a stern discipline. Polygamy was not, therefore, proscribed, nor was marriage indissoluble. This was doubtless an imperfect law, but it was not, as mutual divorce is, contrary to the very nature of society, inasmuch as being accorded to the husband alone, and perhaps without the permission for the woman to remarry, it preserved all the independence of the paternal power, and was an act within its jurisdiction, even when it was not a just act.

Yet this permissiveness, tolerated on account of the hardness of heart of this rude and stiff-necked people, and endurable for a time, concealed—as do all imperfect laws—a seed of corruption that soon germinated. In the books of the rabbis, we see that these doctors, interpreting the law of repudiation according to their whims and the passions of the multitude, permitted the husband to dismiss his wife for the most insubstantial causes and on the most ridiculous pretexts, and even, in the end, as several examples prove, allowed the wife to usurp the right to repudiate her husband.

For several centuries the Romans fought against divorce. It appeared among them only very late. The woman who had had but one husband was always honored. Upon the funerary monuments of ancient Rome may still be read: *Conjugi piae, inclytae, univirae,* or, "To the wife who had but one husband."

Yet the highest wisdom made itself heard, and Christianity, which is but the application to society of every moral truth, began by constituting the family, the necessary element of every public society. It introduced itself into customs. From being voluptuous and cruel, they were made mild and austere. Soon it passed from hearth and home to the throne of the Caesars. It changed the nations as it had changed men, and domestic morals became public laws.

Slow and almost insensible was the progress of that mustard seed, destined as it was to become a great tree uniting all nations under its shade. Slow it was, as is the progress of all things destined for a long life. It was only with great effort that pagan weakness and license were overcome. It is a spectacle worthy of the most serious meditation, that struggle fought by an expiring paganism against the growing influence of the Christian religion. That influence can be perceived in some of the laws of the emperors, even in the first or second century of our era, and it continued even to the last legislators of the Eastern empire. The laws of Justinian are strongly imprinted with it. It is in the wake of all this legislation that we see—with the interest that all great truths inspire in us—society slowly disengaging itself from the errors that had darkened it, and little by little casting out all its barbarous or licentious customs: the exposure of infants, the bloody games of the arena, the sacrifice of human victims, slavery, and divorce, lately become a veritable polygamy. At certain times and in some places, this progress was arrested. Retrograde laws may even occasionally be seen. Yet the general march of society toward civilization was no less constant and continuous, and the peoples of the north, who in the end came to renew the worn-out body of the Roman Empire, received the Christian religion from the vanquished wherever they settled in exchange for the monarchical constitution that they brought to them.

Of all the disorders of paganism, divorce stood out the longest against the influence of the Christian religion. This was not so among the people, whose martial way of life was chaste and simple, but among the great, for whom divorce and even polygamy was a kind of luxury. Tacitus points to this in his *Customs of the Germans,* where he pays due homage to the marriage customs of these peoples. To uproot the habit of divorce as it existed amongst the great required all the authority of the leaders of the Church, employed at times with a rigor that we, far removed from those days, are inclined to tax with imprudence or high-handedness, and of this the history of our kings offers more than one example.

That dangerous permission that Christianity had been at such great pains to banish from society was, in the sixteenth century, reestablished by a Christianity that wished to be more severe, and society was shaken to its foundations. This revolution in the family began and prepared others in the State, and a democratic principle soon manifested itself in the political system of Europe.

The French Revolution, when taking possession of all means of seduction and disorder as if these were its proper patrimony, did not neglect this one. Divorce was decreed. You have seen its ill effects, and you know the disorders that it would have produced if the people—more wise than their legislators—had not opposed their former customs to the new laws, and the severity of their religion and morals to the criminal indulgence of politics. You will doubtless dispense me from recounting the tale for you; time is too dear, and surely, after twenty-five years, it is time to bring the debates to a close.

If, however, you need an authority other than that of your own reason and experience, I should tell you that every time this law was discussed in the Council of State or in the different legislative assemblies, it was opposed by the most honorable men and by the best minds. In time, a writer for whom the worthiness of his cause made up for his want of talent defended it with some success, and it was found to be quicker and easier to insult or proscribe him than to respond to him. I do not fear to say that there appeared neither discourse nor writing in favor of divorce that has left behind a memory. And it is well-known that the usurper himself, at the height of his power, would have abolished it for himself, as he had abolished it for the members of his family, if, seeing himself without posterity, he had not wished to retain the ability to make use of it one day.

The men who introduced it in our laws have always defended it as the seal and the special character of the Revolution. And it has remained in our legislation down to this day, a monument of shame and license that will attest to future centuries of the weakness of morals and the lawlessness of minds in those days.

The difference of religious beliefs about the marital bond cannot be an obstacle to the abolition of divorce.

It cannot be doubted, gentlemen, that the reestablishment of religion is the people's most pressing need, and the first desire of their representatives. Our duty is to restore its standing and influence, to place it once again in the people's habits and sentiments, and to make of it, in a word, the most powerful auxiliary of the administration, just as it is already the fundamental dogma and necessary sanction of every constitution.

Yet in the question that is before you, the government will have fulfilled all its duties toward religion when it will have seen to it that the bond of marriage, formed by the mutual consent of the parties, guaranteed by the civil power, and consecrated by the religious power, cannot be dissolved by law.

Marriage is at once a domestic, a civil, and a religious act, which, in the public state of society, requires for its validity the concurrence of the three powers, domestic, civil, and religious: In the consent of the two parties, authorized by their parents, in the intervention of the civil power, and in the concurrence of the religious authority. Once the bond had been formed by this triple knot, and the family that it has founded has taken its place among the families that compose the State, the legislator should consider it as an integral part, inseparable from the great political whole, composed itself of families, religion, and the State.

Our current laws, separating with so much care what legislators of all times have seen so great an interest in keeping together—religion and politics—consider marriage only as a civil contract, for the validity of which only the consent of the parties is required, without any participation of the religious authority—which the law affects not to recognize—which the law does not permit to precede the civil act that alone causes all the civil effects of marriage.

And on this point, I will be so bold as to speak, in the name of religion and morals, in the name of individual liberty, and even of the liberty of worship, against the tyranny of these unions in which a young girl, betrayed by her own weakness, by the authority of her parents, and at times—and we have seen examples of this—by a higher influence, and engaged only by a civil act, then sees avoided or even formally disavowed the promise of nuptial blessing on the faith of which she had given her hand, without her being able to obtain justice from the perjurer, and thus forced to live in a state that injures public morals as much as her own conscience.

The right of the civil authority to establish impediments to marriage will not, I am sure, be contested. Politics, sometimes more stern than religion, admits some that religion has not been able to recognize. The law in France, for instance, makes an impediment to marriage the parents' lack of consent, a consent that the teaching of the Council of Trent makes a counsel or a duty, but not a legal necessity. And I believe that in Spain, where the teaching of the Council of Trent was received, parental consent was not recognized as necessary until just a few years ago. The Church could also grant dispensations for degrees of prohibited consanguinity that are today prohibited by our laws. Let no one be astonished by this apparent contradiction between religion and politics: Religion is universal, politics is local. Religion, destined to spread to all the nations, and even to newborn nations where procreation is a necessity, had to leave to marriage every facility compatible with the natural law, while the politics of each State, applying the principle to a particular nation, have been able, have even been forced to restrain that facility when a superabundant population bringing together men, women, and families had forced it to place the interest of morals before all others.

It is, therefore, beyond question that the political authority can, for the public interest, of families and of the State, prohibit divorce while allowing separation, and make a pre-existing bond contracted between two persons still living a formal impediment to a second marriage.

Are there, however, sufficient reasons to legitimate this act of the civil power? This is the question before us.

In favor of the indissolubility of the conjugal bond, there are arguments to be drawn from the very physical nature of man, from his moral nature, from the civil law, and from political considerations. We shall briefly address these different matters.

First. The end of marriage is not in the pleasures of the man, for these can be had outside of marriage. Nor is the end of marriage only the production of children, for this effect can take place without marriage. The end of marriage is at once the production of the child and its conservation, a conservation, which, in general, is not secure without marriage or outside of marriage, and, in this word conservation I understand the moral and physical conservation, the care of the child's education as well as of his life.

The end of marriage is, therefore, the perpetuity of mankind, which is composed not of children born, but of children conserved. It has been said that divorce favors an increase in population, but it is forgotten that if the union of the sexes favors the population in an uninhabited land, only the society of the spouses maintains and increases the population in a nation that has been formed; and that divorce, where the legislator has had the imprudence of introducing it or maintaining permission for it, destroys as many families as it gives birth to children. Savage tribes, where all the individuals intermarry, are miserable and weak; and among civilized nations, where the needs of society condemn to celibacy a numerous part of the nation, the State is populous and flourishing.

By divorce women are oppressed no less than are children.

In this society, the original conditions are not equal; the man comes to it with strength and the woman with weakness. Nor, in the case of a dissolution, are the results equal, for the man leaves with all his independence while the woman does not leave with all her dignity, and of all that she brought to it—virginal purity, youth, beauty, fecundity, consideration, fortune—she can regain only her money.

Second. There are moral arguments. Here, gentlemen, allow me to speak to you in the words that when an obscure and proscribed citizen fifteen years ago, I addressed to legislators less worthy than you are to hear them. I will omit several expressions that, happily, no longer apply to the times in which we find ourselves. It is said that the law does not command divorce. "Legislators," I stated,* "among a people less advanced in the arts, the toleration of divorce is without danger because it is without precedent. At that age of society, man sees in a woman only the mother of his children and the governor of his house. His love for her is that of esteem, and hers for him that of respect. Chastity and virginity are honored, and all the refinements of sensibility that present one sex to the other under the relations of personal enjoyment and sentimental affection are unknown to them in their simplicity. Yet when society has come to the point where the headstrong loves of the youth—an inextinguishable nourishment for the arts—have become in a thousand ways the concern of people of every age; when marital authority is the butt of jokes, and paternal authority is thought to be tyrannical; when obscene books, displayed everywhere, sold or loaned at so low a price that you might thought them to be given away, teach the child things that nature does not reveal to the grown man; when human nudity, the distinctive characteristic of extreme barbarism, offers itself everywhere to our eyes in public places, and when the woman herself, clothed without being covered, has discovered the art of insulting modesty without shocking good taste; when religion has lost all its terrors, and when enlightened spouses see in their reciprocal infidelities only a secret to keep from one another, or perhaps a secret to share: In times such as these, to tolerate divorce is to legalize adultery, it is to conspire with man's passions against his reason, and with man himself against society. After this, you may give

---

* EDITOR'S NOTE: In this and the following passages, Bonald was quoting from his *On Divorce* (1801).

garlands of roses to celebrate the virtue of girls, write idylls to celebrate the happiness of spouses, give prizes for fecundity, and put a tax on celibacy, and you will see, in spite of all these philosophical helps, the disorders of voluptuousness grow with the distaste for marriage, and our morals become, if it is possible, as weak as our laws."

At that time, gentlemen, divorce was permitted even for incompatibility of temperament; since then it has been hedged around with more obstacles. Yet it is not a matter of making divorce more difficult, we must make marriage honorable, and not add to all the causes of corruption that act so powerfully within an advanced society that provocation to the natural inconstancy of man to which the indissolubility of the conjugal bond should be the remedy.

Third. If in morals divorce be a source of corruption, in the eyes of the civil law it is an act of injustice, and, if I may say so, this argument seemed conclusive to the famous judge, the late Monsieur Portalis, at whose request the one who is honored to be speaking to you earlier treated the question of divorce.

"The civil power intervenes in the contract of the union of the spouses only because it represents the child that is to be born, the only social object of the marriage, and it accepts the engagement that they make in its presence and under its guarantee to give birth to him. In contracts in general, said the reporter of the project presented to the *Conseil d'Etat,* one speaks for oneself; in marriage, one speaks for another. The power, therefore, speaks for the interests of the child, for the majority of matrimonial clauses are relative to the survival of children, and it even accepts certain particular advantages, spoken of in advance in favor of the child to be born in a certain order of birth or of sex, and ministers to the bond that will give him existence, in order to guarantee the stability that will assure his conservation.

"The conjugal engagement is therefore truly formed among three persons present or represented, for the public power that precedes the family and which survives it always represents within the family the absent person, whether the child before his birth or the father after his death.

"The engagement formed among these three cannot, therefore, be broken by two of them to the prejudice of the third, for this third person is, if not the first, at least the most important; it is to him alone that all refers, and he is the reason for the social union of the two others. The father and the mother who divorce themselves are therefore really two strong parties who conspire to despoil one weak one, and the public power that consents to this is the accomplice to their brigandage. This third person, even if present, can never consent to the dissolution of the society that gave birth to him because he is a minor in the family—even when he has his majority within the State—and consequently always lacks the ability to consent to what is against his interests and to his prejudice. The civil power that represented him when the bond of this society was formed can no longer represent him to dissolve it, because the tutor is given to the pupil not so much as to accept what is useful to him as to prevent his consent to what would injure him."

Fourth. The political arguments for the indissolubility of the conjugal bond are taken from a theory the explanation of which would carry me beyond the bounds of this speech. It suffices to say that such is the identity of principles of the constitution of domestic society and of political society, and such, consequently, is the analogy of our social ideas, that the thoughts, the sentiments, and the habits that give rise to the indissolubility of the domestic monarchy lead naturally to the thoughts, the sentiments, and the habits that defend and preserve the indissolubility—or, what is the same thing—the legitimacy of the political monarchy. All of the doctrines that have weakened the one have weakened the other. Wherever the domestic bond has been dissolved, the political bond has been broken or weakened. Political democracy, which permits the people, the weak part of the political society, to rise up against the power, is the necessary companion of the permission of divorce, the true domestic democracy, that also allows the weak party to rise up against marital authority and to weaken paternal authority. To take the State back from the hands of the people, as Montesquieu said, one must begin by regaining the family from the hands of the women and children.

Do not believe, gentlemen, that it is the Catholic religion or people alone who call for the indissolubility of the conjugal bond: Insistent demands have been raised in the very bosom of the Reform. The question of the abolition of divorce was put to the deliberation of the parliament of England several years ago, and the bishop of Rochester, responding to Lord

Mulgrave, hazarded that for every ten petitions of divorce for the cause of adultery—for in England divorce can be had for no other cause—nine of them have been cases in which the seducer had agreed in advance with the husband to furnish him proof of his wife's infidelity. The same orator remarked that those Englishmen who have shown themselves most indulgent toward divorce were also the most pronounced partisans of French demagoguery. "In England," as Monsieur Malleville has said, "in the name of the court of cassation, divorce has become so abusive that, in spite of the fact that the cost of such an act and procedure is enormous, nevertheless the abundance of gold and the corruption of morals has made adultery and divorce so frequent that in 1779 it gained the attention of the parliament, and some, such as the Duke of Richmond, were of the opinion that it ought to be entirely abolished. They contented themselves, however, with placing new obstacles before it. They prohibited an adulterous man and woman from marrying before the passage of a year; but experience has shown that this remedy has not achieved its object, and recently we have seen the complaints about this subject renewed in parliament."

Protestant writers have at last themselves argued against the permission of divorce. Madame Necker, among others, in a treatise written on this question, admires the doctrine of the Catholic Church on marriage. David Hume, in his eighteenth Essay, says expressly: "The exclusion of polygamy and divorce are sufficient proof of the usefulness of European practices with respect to marriage."

You will doubtless regret, gentlemen, that the severity of your rules will not allow you to pay such striking homage to morals as to vote the abrogation of the permission of divorce by acclamation, and that you are not permitted to treat this disastrous law as the law treats those guilty of public infamy, condemned to the uttermost pain by its name alone.

Let us then hasten, gentlemen, to banish from our legislation this weak and false law that dishonors it. This law is the eldest daughter of the philosophy that has brought revolution the world and destroyed France, and its mother, shameful of its behavior, no longer dares to defend it. This law is rejected by the conscience of the multitudes, disavowed by the morals of all, and is used by those whose dogmas permit it no more often than by those to whom it is prohibited. This law is so weak and so false that the legislators who brought it about, wanting it to be possible, sought nevertheless to make it impracticable, and surrounded it with difficulties and obstacles, not fearing thereby to brand it as criminal even while they were proposing it. The ancients, in an imperfect state of society, more advanced in the culture of arts than in the science of laws, were able to say: "What can laws do without morals?" *Quid leges sine moribus vanae proficiunt?* Yet when the State, having arrived at the final limits of civilization, has taken such a great empire over the family, and when the public power has made off with the whole of the domestic power, the maxim must be reversed, and we must say: "What can morals do without the laws that maintain them, or against the laws which undermine them?"

Let us make bold to say it: The State has no power over the family except to affirm its bond, and not to dissolve it. And if the State destroys the family, the family in its turn will avenge itself and will silently undermine the State. As I said before to the government that then weighed upon our unhappy fatherland:

Alas! We do not deny you the terrible right to annihilate our families by sacrificing to the defense of the State those whom nature has destined to perpetuate it, and who we have raised up with other hopes. Yet we do dispute your right to corrupt them by destroying the authority of the husband, the subordination of the wife, and dependance of the children, and by thus taking away from us the asylum of domestic virtue that protects them from public depravity. And it must be said that you have often encouraged the people in the duty to demand their rights, yet have never spoken to them of the sacred duty of defending their virtues.

Legislators, you have seen divorce bring demagoguery in its path and the dissolution of the family precede that of the State. Let not this experience be wasted, either for our instruction or for our happiness! Families demand morals, and the State demands laws. Reinforce the domestic power, the natural element of public power, and consecrate the entire dependance of women and children, the gauge of the constant obedience of the people.

For twenty years in France men have made laws as weak and transitory as themselves. Declare at last those eternal laws that men do not make and that instead make men; command us to be good, and we will be. A people that has endured all is capable of receiving all. Believe that the era to which society has come no longer permits those weak laws and soft complacencies that suit only its infancy. Misery and shame to the government that would make the social man go back toward the imperfection of the first ages! He would build the edifice of society upon the shifting sands of human passion, and he would sow disorder to leave the following generations to reap revolutions.

And we, gentlemen, a great number of whom are at the end of a career we have barely begun, let us at least leave a lasting monument of so fleeting a political existence in the fundamental law of the indissolubility of the conjugal bond. If the time is wanting for us to fulfill the mission that we have received and accepted, then we will at least have placed the first stone, the cornerstone of the edifice of which others, more fortunate than us, will complete the reconstruction.

We are the first to be confided in about the countless sufferings that the foreign invasion has brought upon our land, and the ministers of the rigorous sacrifices that these have imposed, and we will cause ourselves to be pardoned by our fellow citizens for this dolorous function, and we will be unburdened of it in our own eyes, if we depart having strengthened religion and morals.

I propose that a respectful address be made to His Majesty, to beg him to ordain that all the articles relative to the dissolution of marriage and to divorce, which are contained in chapters 7 and 8 of title V and in chapters 1, 2, 3, 4, and 5 of title VI, be struck from the Civil Code. |•

5 | 1816
On the Proposal to Return the Civil Registers to the Clergy

RELIGION CONSIDERS only three events in the life of man as worthy of being consecrated by her: his entrance into domestic society, his entrance into civil society, and his entrance into eternal society—that is, his birth, his marriage, and his death. By consecrating these, religion takes note of the three acts of the stormy drama we call life. She records them for man, for the Christian, and for herself. Yet politics must also take note of them for itself and for the whole citizenry on account of the numerous relations that bind us to one another in society. It is in itself a matter of indifference whether the registers or public writings that preserve the record of and bear witness to the public nature of these acts be kept by the civil officer or by the minister of religion. What is not, however, a matter of indifference is that there be in society an action that is at once civil and religious and that man be recognized as being both a Christian and a citizen at the same time. For this, one sole officer, religious or civil, must be given the charge of keeping the registers that record the natural and civil estate of men, so that by uniting in the same person, at the same time, and in the same act, the religious and the civil act, society will ensure that man—who is always inclined to free himself from authorities both religious and civil—will be unable to effect the religious act without the civil or the civil without the religious, and thus will be unable to be born, to marry, or to die in a manner hidden from either the Church or the State. As it was impossible to charge the civil officer with the religious act, and, on the contrary, easy and without inconvenience to charge the priest (a man himself and a citizen, even though a minister of religion) with the civil function, our laws preferred to give the custody of the civil registers to the priests. This is an example of the good sense that prevailed in our former laws, or, rather, the good sense that itself shaped them, for these laws, like all good laws, were practiced before they were written down, and the ordinances only regulated the custom and assured its execution.

I have said that the spirit and the reason of our former laws on the manner of recording civil estate was to render inseparable and simultaneous the religious and the civil act. In the current law, and in the abuses to which it has led, may be seen the proof of what I am arguing, and also the proof of man's inclination to separate them and society's desire to reunite them. For, on the one hand, a very large number of spouses, content to have their marriage and the birth of their children witnessed by the civil authority, ask the ministers of religion for neither the nuptial benediction nor the baptism of their children, and they would even be permitted to lay the bodies of their parents to rest in the earth without any declaration to the civil officer if these clandestine burials were not grave dangers which our laws cannot afford to overlook. Many would certainly bury them without any religious ceremony, if the combination of their avarice and sentiment did not keep them attached to the Church's inexpensive burials. Believe me, gentlemen: The man who is being born and the man who dies should be placed under the protection of religious solemnities. Surely there have been unfortunate women, mothers without being wives, who have preserved the life of their child in order to have him baptized. Surely there have been would-be domestic assassins who have spared their victims, fearing lest they betray a false sorrow before the altar and in the presence of the family assembled for the burial.

On the other hand, the law did not separate the civil act from the religious without retaining something of their natural union, and without attributing to the minister of the civil office something of the religious one. For the justice of the peace parodies the ceremonies of religion when he questions the will of the future spouses and has them articulate their reciprocal consent, and, in the language of the law, he offers admonitions and good wishes just as religion does. He receives their vows, and, finally, pronounces the sacramental words and blesses their union. He says to

them, "I join you in the name of the law." Whose law I do not know—
perhaps Robespierre's or Marat's. And by these words alone he gives each a
claim to the other's property. We have ourselves seen this sacrilegious farce
played out in the temples of the capital, before the holy altars, at the feet
of flower-bedecked statues of the most infamous apostles of impiety. We
have also seen the people of those provinces where good sense and good
morals have been preserved walk away from these pathetic ceremonies
filled with horror and disgust, and even prefer to compromise the status of
their children and their prospects for the future than to take part in them.

Finally, gentlemen, nothing is more necessary for the men and families
bound together in society than the publicity of births, marriage, and
deaths. In all of the acts of this kind done by the civil officer, there is a
kind of legal publicity, but there is no real publicity. Our city halls are the
places least frequented by the public. No one goes there to learn who has
been born or who has died, and the signs announcing marriages that are
posted on their doors might as well be entirely hidden.

The church is still the place where the public is most often found in
numbers. The sound of the bells tells the world what is happening, and
either devotion or curiosity attracts the citizenry. And, in spite of the
strong desire, or, let us say, in spite of the fury of the regenerators of
France to keep civil acts free from any intervention on the part of the ministers of religion, they were forced to allow them to publish the banns of
marriage, by which the law informs third parties that may have an interest
in opposing the marriage. We shall say more about this below.

While we are speaking about the interest of third parties, you will note,
gentlemen, as being another proof of the profound good sense of our former legislation, that it held it to be wise and prudent to confide the writing
down of the acts that record the civil estate of men and their families to
those who no longer have a family and are unable to form one, and would
therefore have no direct interest in contesting this condition or disturbing
it. The laws, for instance, held that there might have been a danger in leaving the care of attesting to the precise date of birth of a posthumous child
to the man who by advancing or retarding the day of birth by a single day
might declare him legitimate or illegitimate, according to his interest in the
matter. And that there was a certain inconvenience in confiding the right of

attesting to deaths to a civil officer who might put himself forward as the heir in the very common case in which the mother and the children having died on the same day and almost at the same moment, the predeceasing of one or the other might affect the disposition of the estate.

The act of marriage would seem to be more indifferent. Yet consider, gentlemen, that you have heard of the insoluble difficulties posed by those monstrous unions, made in fear of conscription, between mere youths—almost children even—and the elderly, unions that no priest would have ever blessed, unless he had been forced to. I also know more than one family in which the father, as mayor of the village, has written upon the registers—and always with the same motive—an act of marriage in good and proper form, and before witnesses, of his son with a girl his age, without either one or the other knowing anything about it. And when the two did not wish to ratify the involuntary union, they did not dare complain about it under the reign of the usurper, for fear of sending their father and the witnesses to the galleys; and today, now that the father and the witnesses are dead, they may not ever be able to lodge their complaint.

To these decisive reasons are joined less important considerations of ease and convenience.

In spite of what you have been told about the scarcity of the ministers of religion, there are rural regions in which one is far more likely to be able to find a priest to baptize, to marry, and to bury, than one is the civil officer, distracted as he is by his other duties. This is particularly the case in those places, such as the region in which I live, where several rural villages are grouped together under the authority of one mayor, whose administrative seat is often far away from the isolated homes of the countryside. This makes it very difficult to secure the requisite witnesses.

One is, moreover, more likely to find a cleric who knows how to fill out the civil register than a mayor who knows how to write correctly, and this is especially true in those places where French is not the customary language. I could place before your eyes strange examples of poor or even completely illegible entries in the registers.

One is more likely to gather the necessary witnesses at the moment when the celebrations of the rejoicing families or the funerals call together all the relations to the church, than one would be several days later when the same religious motives do not make a duty of the gathering. And we should also note that the writing down of these acts adds hardly a half-hour to the time necessary to the religious ceremonies, while, in the case of a separate civil act, the countryman whose labors keep him in his fields will likely wait to travel to the far-off city hall until some other business calls him there, and will thus run the risk that the wrong date will be written down for the far more important act.

In our towns, therefore, the ministers of religion are as ready and able as the mayors and their assistants to write down the acts of civil estate, and, in the countryside, they are much more so.

Finally, the registers of civil estate, the most important of all, are more conveniently located and more secure in a sacristy, or even at the priest's rectory, than they are in the communal buildings of the villages, which remain open at all times to passersby, and where they will be mixed together with a host of administrative papers and liable to be subject to accidents and carelessness.

Do not think, gentlemen, that these arguments, and many others that time does not allow me to explain, were unknown to those who during the Constituent Assembly and the bodies that succeeded it took the future of France so boldly in hand. They knew these arguments, but they were convinced—how wise they were!—that it was a more pressing necessity to separate religion and politics. They were men of small minds, the kind that are strongly moved by petty arguments, and they understood neither religion nor politics, believing sincerely, it would appear, that there was imminent peril in leaving them joined together in the way that they had existed in France for so many years. The leaders of this vast conspiracy, better instructed in the reasons for and the effects of this union, and who wished to break the bonds that joined them in order more easily to destroy them when separate, explained themselves more candidly, and the most able among them said openly that France had to be unchurched in order to be unkinged.

In truth, this theocracy against which so many complaints were raised had not prevented France from traversing her long career with an increase—one might even say a venerable increase—of glory, strength, prosperity, and wisdom, in spite of a few passing eclipses, which are as inevitable in the life of States as they are in the course of the planets. Yet we dreamed of a happiness still more complete and of longer duration, and these illusions did not give way before our sophomoric publicists' fascination with antiquity, whose worst institutions they would have revived, even to proscribing Christianity. They were, however, careful not to recall Rome's religious spirit, which, in spite of the idolatry of the day, was, as Montesquieu put it, like an anchor holding fast the ship amidst the storm and giving a certain stability to a most imperfect political constitution.

As we have been led onto this topic, I will not hesitate to speak about that confusion of the civil and religious powers that has been held up as a kind of scarecrow for so long. The first one who said "the Church is in the State, not the State in the Church" spoke utter nonsense, for if by the Church he meant its temples, ministers, disciples, and possessions, then it is plain that all of the material of religion, which might be thought of as its body, must of physical necessity be found within the limits of the territory of the State, just as the State itself is in the world, and as every body exists within a determinate time and place. But if by the Church he understood religion, its teaching, its creed, its sacraments, its graces, and so forth, then he committed a grave error. If the Church, in the material sense, is in the State, then society is in religion, because in religion and in religion alone does it discover the supreme justification for power and the final justification for duty and obedience, and the very text of the fundamental laws that regulate the exercise of power and the mode of obedience. And because, finally, outside of religion and without religion one cannot explain why one commands and another obeys, and, one would perceive in the world only the abuses committed by the strong and the sufferings of the weak.

The Church is, therefore, in the State, and it is for this reason that the State protects it and that it can protect it. But society is in religion and exists by religion, and it is for this reason that religion defends society against the passions.

If man is, as has been said, an intellect served by organs, then society is nothing other than religion served by politics for the happiness—even temporal happiness—of man, the unique goal of all politics as of all religion. Politics doubtless must not make into a law all that religion teaches by way of precept, and the same is true reciprocally. But the one should not prohibit what the other ordains, or still less, render it impossible. When thinking about politics, therefore, one must think as a religious man, and, conversely, when thinking about religion one must think as a statesman. They have been separated far too much and must from now on be joined together without being confounded.

I return to the question before us, in order to examine the objections that have been made against the proposal of our honorable colleague.

In opposition to the proposal have been adduced the beliefs of non-Catholics and even of non-Christians, and by these I mean the Jews, because in a Christian society only the Jews have the sad privilege of existing within the social body without being Christians. Yet the present law on the custody of the civil registers changed nothing in the manner in which non-Catholics and non-Christians were to record their births, marriages, and deaths. The law that would return to the former usage would leave them in the same condition. If they wish to have these acts recorded by the ministers of their own cult, it would be just to leave them free to do so. We must even desire that they do so. And as to the objection that the non-Catholics do not have ministers everywhere, it would be easy to reply that they do have elders who, according to their own practice, take the place of ministers and could fill out the registries just as well as the mayor's assistant could.

Here, gentlemen, I must rebut the reproach of intolerance with which you have been so unjustly charged. The only necessary intolerance that I know of is the kind of public secularism advocated by Jean-Jacques Rousseau. I profess to regard the unity of religion—which must not be sought outside of the religion of unity—as the first of all political interests. Political practice seems to agree, for the chief cause of political disorder in States has been the promotion of religious dissension, a terrible cause of harm that should be prohibited among Christians, just as soldiers should not be allowed the use of poisoned weapons. But though my views seem paradoxical, I will say that I see no more sure means of returning the world to the unity of belief than by each adhering to his own belief with sincerity. Faith studies, seeks, and chooses; doubt grows in the soil of indifference. This is the great political evil done to France by the irreligious writings of the past century: that by sowing a general indifference toward religion, they stopped the progress of a reunion of the churches that was already more well-advanced than is generally known, and substituted for it a worldly honor that glorified too much in its own self-satisfaction to fulfill the duty of enlightening oneself about the most important subject for life and for society.

You have been told of the appeals by the royal courts against abuses by the clergy, of the refusal of sacraments, of the pretensions of the popes, and even of the constitution *Unigenitus.** These are superannuated concerns, the memory of which is cherished, ridiculously, only in Paris, and not in the provinces. I will admit that I see many other kinds of abuses against which one might appeal, and say further that the many constitutions that have succeeded one another in France since 1793 have made me lose sight of the constitution *Unigenitus.* After what we have seen, and at the place where we have arrived, to speak of these miseries—I almost said of these amusements—that belong to our time of happiness, is to act like the landowner who has lost his land but still complains about the hard work that the upkeep of his possessions occasioned him in the past. Abuses can occur in the execution of even the best of laws, just as there is always some miscalculation or other in even the most well-kept accounts, but I shall not cease repeating that, in politics, one must not be distracted by the abuses of good institutions or by the advantages of bad ones. If it is an abuse to refuse Christian burial to someone, it is an evil, and a great evil, to have passed one's entire life scandalizing one's neighbors. If it is an abuse to refuse the last assistance of the Church to those who ask for it, it is an evil, and a great evil, not to defer to a legitimate authority. The quarrels between the Church and the State are, doubtless, an evil, but the profound indifference for religion and for the fate of one's land is a still greater evil. Many people will say to you, and perhaps say it in good faith, when certain measures are proposed, that the time or men are not ready for such changes. They should like the reestablishment of order to precede the means of reestablishing it, and the healing to take place before the remedy is administered. Is it possible in France to do what has been done

---

* EDITOR'S NOTE: The Apostolic Constitution *Unigenitus Dei Filius* (1713) of Pope Clement XI condemned propositions taken from the writings of Pasquier Quesnel. An episode in the long history of Jansenism, *Unigenitus* touched off a particularly damaging episode of dissent within the French Church.

elsewhere, to restore the custody of the civil registers to the ministers of religion? Yes, they must be returned to them. Difficulties and inconveniences are everywhere to be found, and, it would certainly be strange if we allowed ourselves to be hindered in our pursuit of the good by some difficulties, when, in order to do evil, we French have done the impossible. Nothing is easier than to do the good: The hard part is to will it.

We have put forward—or, we at least believe that we have put forward—strong arguments, and we could have adduced powerful examples. In neighboring lands, ones that were quite recently subject to French laws—Lombardy among others—the government has hastened to return to the former customs and to give back the task of keeping the acts of civil estate to the ministers of religion. Many petty arguments have been raised against us, but in the balance of politics, many petty arguments do not weigh as much as one strong one. We must save our petty arguments for our petty domestic interests, our petty fears, our petty worries. But when we are dealing with society—that which is of the greatest importance—we must consider only the most important interests and decide them only according to the purest motives.

What is most urgent of all, and what cannot wait, is to restore peace to individual consciences and to families, first, by regarding as valid those marriages contracted before the civil officer when they have been followed by cohabitation, and as null, on the other hand, those contracted before the civil officer, which were not followed by cohabitation and which the two parties both refused to consummate, and, second, by requiring the intervention of the religious authority for the validity of all unions.

At this point, gentlemen, allow me to say that we have hitherto paid insufficient attention to the natural reason for the authority of religion over the bond that the spouses contract.

In the union of man with woman, there are three things to consider: the marriage, which is the physical union between the sexes and is formed by the free and mutual consent of the parties; the society, a moral bond, a bond of wills that religion alone can effect by the empire that it enjoys over our wills; and the family, entirely civil or political, the integral part of the great civil and political body of the State, which the State admits into its being, and of which, consequently, it should approve the foundation and recognize the existence. It was by taking one for the other—marriage, society, family—or by having considered them separately, or by not having distinguished the original and necessary condition of marriage from its subsequent but equally necessary condition in civilized society, that theologians and even publicists have made different systems about the essence and the nature of the conjugal bond.

Thus in every union (if this word can be thus employed) where the free consent of the parties is lacking—the fundamental condition of every union and the prime matter of every bond, religious and civil—there is neither marriage, nor society, nor family. The uniting of the sexes without consent is, consequently, a violation punishable by law.

Where there is consent of the parties without the religious or the civil bond, there is marriage, but in a civilized State there is neither society nor a recognized family. Neither the moral nor the political bond is present. This is the condition that we call concubinage, and it is condemned both by nature and by law.

Where there is consent of the parties and the religious bond without the civil one, there is marriage between the sexes and society between the spouses, but the State is not able to recognize a family.

Finally, in the case of consent between the parties and a civil bond without the religious one, there is marriage and family, but religion cannot recognize a true society.

The fact of the consent of the parties is expressed by common habitation, or, legally, by a contract. The religious bond is formed by the priest's blessing. The civil authority, in the past, intervened only by the publication of the banns.

The banns are the act by which the civil power, making use of the ministers of religion and of the day set aside for religion in order to add to the solemnity of the proceedings, announces to the public—that is, to the other families that compose the State—the intention of the man and the woman to found a new family, and consequently to begin sharing the civil rights of their elders. The authority asks the other citizens whether the man and the woman are free to unite themselves, that is, whether they have not earlier contracted an engagement with other families and other persons that precludes their forming a new bond. And it warns them to watch over any interests that might be damaged by the domestic arrangements of the new family, for we know that third parties may often have an interest in opposing a marriage. If there is no opposition, the silence of the other citizens is taken to signify their consent. If some opposition arises, either on the part of creditors, or on the part of persons with whom the future spouses would be bound by promises anterior to marriage, or even on the part of those who might have had knowledge of some public or secret obstacle that should render the marriage null and impossible, the religious bond cannot be formed before the civil authority has allowed the celebration of the marriage to proceed, and has assured itself, against the new family, of the honor and the interests of the older ones. Note that in this circumstance, the civil authority precedes the religious one without offending its dignity or injuring its discipline. And, for its part, the grateful religion levies the most stern penalties upon those who by a guilty silence or false accusation would deceive the wisdom of the civil authority and without a legitimate justification maliciously contest the establishment of a new family.

This was the general condition of the laws governing marriage in Europe until the fifteenth century and in France until the eighteenth.

In the fifteenth century, some theologians lacking all knowledge of politics took away from marriage its sacramental character, recommending the continued intervention of the minister of the cult, but only as an act of piety and of deference toward religion. In the eighteenth century, irreligious politicians, wishing to avoid even naming religion for fear of being obliged to acknowledge its claims, gave to the purely civil bond the strength that others had taken away from the religious bond. Both of them, in forming marriage and even families, destroyed society. If all they had wished had been to establish the liberty of worship, they could have left to the members of their own communions the duty to bless their marriages according to their own rites. Yet they wanted to destroy all of them equally, and they wanted the dissolubility of marriage. For this double project, it was necessary to banish from this great act of human life any and all intervention by religion, and thence it became indispensable to consider marriage as only the acquisition that a man makes of a woman by a contract similar to that by which he might acquire anything else. The woman belonged to the man, and was not of the man. The man was no more united to the woman he had espoused than to the house in which he lived and which he might change at whim for a more convenient one.

It was in the name of liberty, equality, and the rights of man that these madmen—today more worthy of our compassion than our anger—began by introducing into the family the disorders that would soon penetrate the State, and by placing the cruel inequality of divorce between man and woman and its inevitable effects between fathers and children, condemned woman to slavery, children to abandonment, and man to the torment of his own unlimited inconstancy and unbridled passions. It was in the name of a future happiness, the brilliant chimera of which they held up before our eyes, that they came bearing hardship for our consciences, and violated all our sentiments, and by these laws that were disrespectful of religion, took away from scrupulous man his heart's peace, the only refuge that remained to him amidst the misfortune of public discord.

In order more effectively to erase from the mind and heart of the people every religious idea and sentiment, and to replace the solemn ceremonies that the religion of their fathers had used for marriages, the city official, as we have already said, was made to parody those rites. He had the spouses appear together; he received their promises; he spoke sacramental words, and thus he united by the law of man those who had hitherto been united by the law of God.

Yet the greatest evil of these false institutions—an evil as contrary to the politics of the State as to the religion of the State—is the situation in which they have placed a large number of families in which the young spouses, bound only by the civil act, sometimes have not been able—and I know examples of this—and more often have not been willing to receive the nuptial blessing, and have lived until the present apart from one another, such that there is neither marriage—for the refusal to live together is either a denial or a formal retraction of the necessary consent—nor society, inasmuch as there is no moral or religious bond, nor even a family.

Sometimes it has even happened that a young girl, raised in a profound ignorance of the civil law and its effects, but instructed in her religion, has presented herself for the civil act wishing and believing herself to do nothing other than to save from conscription a young man in whom her family had taken an interest, and she had regarded the nuptial benediction as necessary and indispensable to any real marriage.

More likely still, betrayed by her own weakness, she has handed herself over upon the assured hope and formal promise that the religious act would soon complete the civil one, to consecrate the commitment and to ratify the union. And today, unworthily deceived by a villain who has become her husband without being her spouse, and she a woman, and sometimes even a mother, without being able to believe herself to be a spouse, she lives in a condition that injures both her honor and her conscience.

Take note, gentlemen, that the law owes equal protection to all citizens, and that in such a case there is an evident injustice and a real oppression caused by one of the parties, who, having received the commitment of the other party in the civil act, refuses, on her request, to commit himself in the religious act.

It is plain, for instance, that the woman who by the civil act has committed her dowry to her future spouse, and has received in exchange the commitment of the other to join to it his own possessions or the fruit of his labors, has not attempted to make a distinction between his person from his possessions, nor has his spouse separated hers from herself. And if she believes that the two *persons* cannot be committed to one another except by the nuptial blessing, she is, most rigorously entitled to demand her spouse to accomplish his part of a commitment whose price she has already paid. One cannot conceive of a more miserable condition than that of a woman who has handed over her possessions without being able to follow them herself, nor a more unjust one than the refusal of the man who has received them to receive the gift of the person.

A law would therefore be unjust and barbarous if it began by placing the goods of the woman at the disposition of her husband and refused to her the only act by which the woman could believe that the person of the husband has been committed to her own, and reciprocally. Yet this is what happens today in these unions that are consented to upon the promise that they would later be consecrated by religion, but which too often remain undone.

This disorder, which has already been brought to an end in the States neighboring France, cannot be tolerated any longer in our laws. |•

6 | 1815–1817
Opinions Pronounced in the Chamber of Deputies

Selections from the Legislative Sessions
of 1815–1816 and 1816–1817

On the Restoration of Unsold Church Lands[1]

YESTERDAY THE proposal was made to return to religion the unsold part of its possessions. I say to religion, and not to the clergy, for, while we would willingly see the ministers of the altar live in decent comfort, it is religion alone that we wish to endow and to enrich. We must not be misled on this point. The possessions of the clergy were the effect of the piety of the faithful, but the wealth of religion that founded and supported so many useful institutions was, more than one generally thinks, the cause of that piety.

The proposed measure tends to return France, on an important point, to the territorial or landed system that she so unfortunately abandoned in favor of the fiscal system. The latter is a brilliant system, it is true, but it lacks solidity, and by excessively favoring a movement that was mere motion, it has made our habits inconstant and our minds unsteady.

Religion, like royalty, became a landowner, and did so in the earliest times, to the extent that it passed from the precarious condition of a persecuted doctrine to the fixed and stable condition of a society. Yet both in her early days, when she lived by the gifts that her disciples made to her, and subsequently, when she received or acquired landed properties, she held her property in custody for her people.

These donations were neither the work of one age, nor of one man, nor of one law. A great and religious thought inspired every mind, a general motive impelled every particular motive, even when they were not terribly well enlightened, and each one obeyed, without knowing it, the general directive, thinking that he was taking counsel only from himself, when he was led on by the force of things and a universal cast of mind.

I know as well as any other the abuses that slipped in, and will again be able to slip in if the right to acquire land is restored to the clergy. "If," said Montesquieu, "I wanted to recount the abuses of the most necessary institutions, I could say abominable things." Allow me to repeat the first axiom of the science of society: "One should never allow one's gaze to rest upon abuses that are inseparable from better things, nor upon the advantages—which may be called inevitable—that one encounters in the worst things."

Our fathers witnessed the disorders caused by the misuse of ecclesiastical property by a few ministers of religion even more than we have, but they did not accuse religion of the faults of its ministers any more than they did royalty of the faults of their kings. It was reserved to the philosophy of our days to restrict our vision by always seeing man and never society.

These large gifts strengthened the constitution of the State even as they marvelously aided the administration. The credit of these large bodies was a valuable resource during public crises, and their wealth a help in times of need. In every political crisis, the clergy contributed from its possessions. It paid the ransom of François I, and it offered, at the beginning of the Revolution, four hundred million francs to pay off the deficit, which, still today, and with greater financial resources, would solidify France's fortunes and bring stability to her government. Its vast possessions, distributed throughout every province, were veritable granaries of abundance for the poor, who we will always have with us no matter what we do, and to whom today we are unable to give bread except by depriving them of their liberty in order to prevent them from asking for it.

The large properties of the Crown and of religion had the immense political advantage of moderating the excesses of an always growing population, and to furnish, by the abundance of their produce, the consumption of that populous class that, not cultivating the earth, can live only by the surplus production of large properties.

The political revolution that began in the fifteenth century attacked every part of this beautiful system, discovered in the woods, as Montesquieu said, and against which the ignorance and greed of the cities was raised. This war, fought for three centuries, sometimes by arms, sometimes by writings, and under different banners, was brought to an end by the Revolution, that vast tidal wave in which perished religion, morals, the State, families, laws and customs, communities and their possessions, in a word, everything.

Then the ancient social economy was overturned, and the fiscal system prevailed over the system of landed property. Already for a long time favored by public credit, it manifested itself in the family by the trend of converting family properties into rents upon the State. The State, in its turn, converted public properties into taxes upon the family.

Then the public treasury, that is, taxes paid by private individuals, had to fund the royal household, the military, the courts, the Church, public instruction, and even public charity. Everything that had been a benefit for society became an expense for the people, and the great book of public debt will soon be the only public property left to a great many governments. Soon the governments of agricultural peoples will no longer be rooted to the soil. Instead of being large property owners, they will be nothing other than large exacters of contributions.

Against Clerical Membership in the Chamber of Deputies[2]

I would not have clergy admitted [to the Chamber of Deputies], at least insofar as they are not landowners. The ministers of religion, like religion itself, should not be found except where they are the first or the last, for there is no dignity for them other than in power or in suffering. Thus the nature of things would have it. Ministers of religion mixed into political assemblies and solicited in contradictory ways by all of those who would seek their votes would soon lose all their consideration. I cannot accustom myself to the idea of a bishop presenting himself on the ballot with a neighbor from a country village and not being chosen over him. It is by the exercise of their ministry that priests can affect our good choices, by warning the people against their own passions and those of others. Let it not be said that there will be no one in our political assemblies to defend the interests of religion. We will all be there to do it, for it falls to us to defend it, inasmuch as it is made for our sake. It is here that we must invoke the maxim:

"My kingdom is not of this world." Religion is outside of the world only in order better to govern our minds, and it should not descend from the throne to mix itself in the crowd of those who administer our affairs.

A Protest Against the Sale of Common Lands[3]

Yet after all, gentlemen, what are we arguing about? Do the possessions of the communes and of religion belong to the King? Do they belong to us, to dispose of them generously, as we doubtless would? Surely we do not forget that the King is not the owner of his entire domain, for he is not the owner of even his particular domains, but the guardian of every interest. Nor do we forget that the nation is the pupil, and that we, under every form of our political existence, from Estates-General to *parlement* to legislative assemblies, we, legitimately elected, we are (I do not hesitate to insist upon the comparison) the family council that must agree with the guardian, and even, when money is in question, to authorize by our consent the payment in this or that manner of the expenses of the pupil, whose perpetual minority does not allow us to authorize ourselves to do anything against his interests.

I understand that the property of the émigrés has been sold. The terrible maxim *vae victis*, the first line in the pagan law of nations, "that took from the vanquished," as Montesquieu has said, "their possessions, their wives, their children, their temples, and even their tombs," that hateful abuse of force that the Christian religion banished from the modern law of nations, was brought back by the Revolution.

I understand the sale of the property of religion in a time when, to minds fascinated by detestable maxims, it was painted as the work of lies and as an instrument of oppression.

I understand the sale of the possessions of royalty: Whether one wished the Crown dependent or not to exist at all, it followed that it must be reduced to receiving from the nation a salary that could be suspended or entirely suppressed at whim.

But the communes, what crime could have been imputed to them?* What reproach could have been made to them? The communes did not

---

* EDITOR'S NOTE: By "communes" Bonald means the 30,000 or more rural villages in France.

emigrate, and, surely, no one thought of destroying them. These little domestic States were the elements of the public State. They were Celtic before they were Gallic, Gallic before they were Roman, Roman before they were French, and they still preserved in their names the vestiges of their ancient origin or of the successive changes in their rule. The communes existed before the monarchy. They existed without the State, and the State could not have existed without them. Since the origin of the State, they have acquitted themselves of their portion of men for wars or public service, and their allotment of money for taxes, and thus purchased, at the price of their children's blood and sweat, the right to be protected by the public power. They have also received from our kings the benefit of their freedom, and it was the usurper who plunged them into servitude again by stripping them of their common property, which properly constituted their community, and without which there was nothing common among the inhabitants of the same place other than what is common to all of the inhabitants of the globe: the air we breathe. The civil authority in France does not have, at any time and under any form of government, any more right to dispose of the possessions of the communes than the communes themselves have to dispose of the possessions of private individuals, nor than the province has to sell a commune, or the State a province. And without contesting the mission of the last Chamber of Deputies, we may be assured that it did not have, and that it could not have received from the communes, the authorization to alienate their properties. Moreover, though it hardly needs saying, it would be difficult to find in the Charter of June 25, 1814, the authorization necessary to sell the properties, even the national ones, that its ninth article had declared inviolable, and inviolable, no doubt, in the hands of those who possessed them when the Charter was granted; for the communes, like the émigrés, were dispossessed only by completed sales, and not by the mere decree. In this regard the Charter confirmed what had been done, and not what was to be done.

I bid you to recall the universal horror that filled the capital and the kingdom when the law of March 20, 1813, was proposed that stripped the communes of their properties. The scandal of it was shocking, even after so many scandals. We were ourselves witness to the profound sadness and even shame of the deputies of the *Corps législatif,* the majority of whom admitted that they could not dare to return to their provinces if they had been so weak as to consent to this monstrous iniquity. You know of the resources that were brought into play. The supporters of the tyranny employed every argument, promise, and threat at their disposal. The tyrant himself momentarily feared that he would not succeed, and, for the first time, he counted, trembling with rage, seventy-five opponents. That day they were the true Frenchmen, and some of them plainly showed the black ball before they dropped it into the urn in the presence of the ministers of State. And now, after the return of the legitimate authority, under the reign of Louis XVIII, and in the presence of that beneficent race whose ancestors set free the communes, it has been proposed that we despoil them!

On the Corporate Representation of Rural Communes[4]

The commune, I repeat, is the political element of a monarchical nation, the veritable political family. It is with the constitution of the commune, or its emancipation, that France attained the regular and best-determined form of the constitution of the State.

The commune, if I may be allowed the comparison, is to the political system what the franc is to the monetary. It is the first and generating unit, the indivisible unit, because one cannot divide it without falling into valueless fractions, monies lacking either heft or name.

And note, gentlemen, that the commune is a more real, more solid, and more visible body than is the *département** or the kingdom, which are, rather, moral bodies. The man, the house he inhabits, the land he cultivates: These belong to the commune before they belong to the *département* or the kingdom. As these three bodies—commune, *département*, kingdom—form the political body, or the State, whole and entire, it is perfectly natural that, in the manner of composing the universal representation of the nation, these bodies themselves participate, in the same order, in the choice of the deputies. Thus when the commune delegates to the *département*, and the *département* delegates to the kingdom, there is an analogous and complete

---

* EDITOR'S NOTE: The *départements* were the administrative divisions of the kingdom imposed by the Constituent Assembly in 1790. Originally 83 in number, they are in size roughly analogous to American counties.

system of elections. This is the justification for the two degrees of election that reason approves, politics counsels, and the Charter allows.

Certainly, gentlemen, you will not accuse me of favoring those popular systems that are as far removed from my tastes as from my principles. You will see momentarily what I would have the commune's choice of deputies consist in. Yet, in partially reducing its franchise, I would not—as does the proposed law—reduce it to naught. An inhabitant of the countryside myself, I respect it—and without closing my eyes to its vices—as being an asylum of sincere morals, of innocent labors, frugal living, and moderation in desires, and as the nursery of our cities and of our families that sometimes recalls the happiness of the earliest ages to hearts oppressed by the disorders of recent times. I myself also love the corporations, of which the commune is the first and the most natural, and the only one that has survived the destruction of all the others. These were also to be found in the forests of Germany. There were both communes and corporations there, inasmuch as there was deliberation. "This beautiful system of government," of which the commune is the foundation, "was found in the woods," as Montesquieu said. In this regard I fully share both the opinion and the regrets of our honorable colleague Monsieur de Serre. I would like to see in the provinces some political beings other than electors with a hundred *écus*. If the States where the municipal power was more developed have appeared so weak against the course of events, as was argued by Monsieur de Serre's opponent, it is because the municipal power should only be applied to the commune, and that among the peoples of whom he spoke, it was applied to the State, the unformed assemblage of every popular mode of government, and that these States were in the last analysis nothing but large municipalities. Did the most powerful monarchies defend themselves any better?

It was, therefore, upon the invariable and unshakable foundation, on an element as indestructible as is every element, upon the commune, which preceded governments and which has survived them, that we must place the first stone of the edifice of a truly national representation. This is the true and only means of establishing the representation of the nation, and of implanting representation within the constitution and the constitution in the State.

Nothing could be more simple than this theory. Each commune should be considered as a single property owner and, within it, each landowner should have similar rights and dignity. This will honor the nation even in its most humble children, and raise up in the eyes of each citizen the importance of the corporation to which he belongs. In this way a kind of political equality will be established among all the communes, just as there is a certain natural equality that exists among all men. In the eyes of reason and of virtue, a forgotten commune, still unstained by the Revolution and its injustices, where the most lively affections for religion and the royalty are preserved under its thatched roofs, is as much as a part of the State as are those opulent cities, which contain the whole fortune of the nation, and which have so poorly guarded the treasures confided to them.

There is, moreover, less inequality among communes than one might suppose, if one considers the landed property as the primary basis of representation. Large cities are mostly populated by men without property of any kind, and manufacturing towns, with a greater population, count fewer owners of landed property than do agrarian communes. Nor does politics admit of any difference between the diplomatic representation of the largest States and the smaller ones, as all are represented in foreign nations by one ambassador alone.

With a theory so simple, so true, and so natural, there are no difficulties of execution to be raised. Nature gives man's reason principles in their simplicity, just as she gives to his industry the primary materials for the useful arts, and she leaves to him the care of applying the principles to society's needs, and brute material to his own needs.

The system of communes—although disfigured by the dominant ideas of personal individuality—counted for something in the establishment of the primary assemblies of the canton and electoral district. It was preserved with all of its faults in the last electoral system to be presented in the previous session. It would have sufficed to regularize it, and to return to its principles in order to have a first round of elections that would be truly political. Yet the authors of the law that is now before you rejected it entirely. We have buried ourselves, more than at any other stage of our errors, in the false and dangerous principle of individuality; and the communes, enfranchised by the absolute monarchy, have been disinherited by the constitutional monarchy.

The Charter has been appealed to, as if the Charter had abolished the right of communes, and as if it could have abolished it.

Where, I wonder, are we to find in the Charter the suppression of the electoral colleges of the districts, when, in article 35, we read that "The Chamber of Deputies will be composed of the deputies elected by the electoral colleges." The Charter does not say of the *département* or of the district, it says the "electoral colleges," and the electoral colleges of the district were at that time still involved in elections, just as were the electoral colleges of the *départements*. Every college that elects is an electoral college; and since the promulgation of the Charter, the district electoral colleges have been convoked in both elections to have taken place. If the Charter had wished to take from the district electoral colleges the right to vote that they had formerly possessed, then it would have avoided all equivocation, and indicated, by name that the electoral colleges of the *départements* were the only ones to be preserved. The proof that the Charter did not intend to suppress them is that immediately after, in articles 36 and 37, it retains everything that was possible to retain, even the number of deputies that the *départements* had at that time, and even with the same length of terms.

Did the Charter suppress the local electoral assemblies at the same time as it consecrated and guaranteed so many institutions that are far less useful, far less respectable, and much more burdensome for the State? Did it give exclusively to private individuals who pay three hundred francs in taxes the right to vote that it stripped from the communes, which altogether pay thirty times as much in taxes? The right to vote is a shared right and not an individual one: It belongs to the community, not to the individual. The Charter did not wish, and could not take away, the commune's right of representation in order to transmit it to the individual. It is the community alone, whether a commune or a *département*, that has the right to representation, and it exercises it through the election of the deputy she has chosen to defend her interests.

On the Evils of Administrative Centralization[5]

We cannot enough insist upon the need to be sparing in our administration, less because a bloated administration will ruin us than because it will corrupt us. In a State, everything rises up to meet the level of a profligate administration. The State becomes profligate in its representation, profligate in the work that it takes upon itself, profligate in the number of agents its employs and the affairs that it attracts to the center and to the capital—where the employees must be paid for their pleasures, which are even more expensive than their services. Every bit of business comes to Paris. Men come there in pursuit of their affairs, and the men are followed by their fortunes. The provinces are depopulated of capable men and impoverished. As in a conquered land, there is no more authority unless what follows from the consideration for the poor, and pride—having nothing better to do—seeks an outlet in a luxury beyond its means, because it is no longer ruled by its condition. That most precious treasure of a people, men of substance and reputation, is wasted. All that remains are wealthy men evaluated by the taxes they pay, like common beasts by the amount of wool they produce. It may be said that such is the spirit of the age, and that we must conform to progress. In Tacitus's day, too, men spoke of the spirit of the age: the morals of despotism that had concentrated in Rome all the world's business and vice. We must, however, return to other morals or perish. Something must be done with the provinces, if a kingdom is to be made out of them. This much-vaunted centralization, ruinous for the administration, and a mortal wound to politics, serves only to enlarge a city that is already too large, to enrich its inhabitants, and to destroy the nation. The most resistant and most stable country in Europe is the one in which each province is a kingdom, each market town a capital, and where the king is everywhere—like God upon our altars—*a real presence*. In the machine of the State, when the movement is fixed at the center, it ceases at the extremities. This is the same way that life comes to an end in animate beings. A State must have centralized surveillance. Every other centralization, whether of opinions, administrative expertise, or, especially, of public instruction, has never served, and will never serve anything but revolutions, which, expanding from the center to all of the parts, have the newspapers for their dispatches and the telegraph for their courier.

On the Conservation of Forests[6]

Forests can never be likened to any other kind of property. They are the cradle of a people at its birth, the asylum of a people in time of trial, and the most precious treasure of a people well-ruled. All of society's arts, all of life's needs demand their conservation because they require their use. Civilization itself demands it, for if one were to suppose a total lack of combustibles in a large country, it is not to be doubted that the rawness of food alone would suffice to reduce the people to a state of barbarism.

There, gentlemen, is the profound reason for the interest that every nation has placed in the conservation of a resource—the daughter of time rather than the work of man, independent in some sense from nature herself, inasmuch as it grows in spite of infertile land and inclement weather— a resource which society cannot do without, yet one which society tends ceaselessly to diminish.

Every people has made of their forests more a public domain than a common one, as the seas and the rivers are. Idolatrous peoples made their temples of them. The pagans consecrated them to their divinities—and the many places called *Le Luc* in the south of France where the Roman tongue is better preserved still testify to the existence of these sacred groves, called *Lucas.* The moderns, instructed in another school, have made them the prerogative of their public establishments, of royalty, religion, or even of the nobility and the communes, in a word, the corporations that were able best to defend them and had the least need to alienate them, or the persons who attached to their conservation ideas of luxury and pleasure more powerful to conserve them even than ideas of personal utility.

The forests, in the hands of these possessors, were placed under the protection of an inalienability that would conserve for all generations a good that belonged to all and of which each had the use. Such was the importance that the administration attached to this kind of property that the private individual himself was not the owner of it in same way as he was of his other possessions, for the use that he made of them was subject to the regulations of the forestry administration.

These forests, spread about the provinces, were all of the public domain, and, consequently, as with everything public, the domain of the poor. Whether custom or law allowed him to take what liberal nature left scattered there, or whether beneficence closed its eyes upon the petty theft that justice could neither punish nor pardon, the poor man had in the forest a support of his life as necessary as his very bread, because the making of his bread depended upon it.

I ask you, gentlemen: If France had an enemy keen to destroy her, seeking at all costs the means to injure her material estate as she has herself injured her moral and political estate, would he dry up the rivers that water the provinces, or stop up the seas that bathe her coasts, or strip the soil's fertility or the air's salubrity? No, he would sell her forests, her only remaining public property, certain that man's petty works would soon squander these vast workshops of nature, and that, to gain one day's bread from them, he would forever ruin the productivity destined to support generations for ages to come.

And what, gentlemen, is the generation that can claim a right to dispose of a wealth that belongs to every generation, of a possession that the generations of French who have preceded us have transmitted to us in order that we might transmit it in our turn to the generations who are to follow, of a possession that belongs as much to the public domain as to the private? Do note, gentlemen, that there is no forest in which either private individuals or communes fail to have, either by law or immemorial custom, rights that truly belong to them, as inviolable a kind of property as all of those that the Charter consecrates and guarantees. Upon the faith in this enjoyment, families are fixed, villages are built, countries are populated, just as men have placed themselves on the banks of rivers, or at the seaside, or near springs. It is fire and water that the Creator has given to men, and that justice has the right to take away only from the condemned.

When a murderous industry has stripped the earth of its most lovely finery, and society of its most useful property, nature will revenge herself. She will chase man from a domain he has made desolate. The land will be depopulated, and, in the absence of the faithless colonist, nature will silently raise up again those vast forests that will one day receive a new population.

The forests conserve the population in two opposing manners. They furnish necessities to the existing population, and, by reducing the amount of soil that is cultivated, they prevent an excessive growth of the population, which would be inevitably followed by a general depopulation. Note also that the forests almost all grow in places with light and sandy soil, which, quickly exhausted by the plough, soon serves only for the forage of animals.

While France is perishing from the division of landed properties—which is a constant cause of the growing dearness of necessities, and which will cause us all to die of hunger when each of us has his one acre to cultivate—you would like to compound this morselization by the sale of the great tracts of forests that remain to us. I cannot, I admit, bring myself to understand this luxury of destruction; like the great scoundrels of antiquity, we seem to be agitated by a sacred fury that forces us to rip ourselves apart with our own hands, and to accomplish the prediction of one of our greatest ministers: "France will die for lack of wood."

If, gentlemen, you doubt the necessity of conserving your forests for the needs of the population, you will have but to consider the increase in price of every kind of necessary good, especially wood for heating and construction, compared to the decrease in price of many manufactured and luxury objects, and this only since the days of Louis XIV. You will see the proof of this in the enormous growth of the industrial population, which has caused manufactured objects to be made more quickly, and consequently in greater quantity, and in the more stationary condition of the agricultural population, obliged to furnish the subsistence of a laboring class much more numerous than before, and to furnish it even when that class cannot earn it.

The price of wood becomes excessive wherever nature has not placed coal mines nearby, but, even where wood can be found, it only serves to delay the time when half the population is forced to bury itself alive in the bowels of the earth to furnish the needs of the other half. Happy the land where nature has not placed the necessities of so fleeting and so troubled a life at so high a price!

Finally, to consider the sale of forests under a more general and more truly political heading: The forests are the last refuge of the people who inhabit the plains. All those who exist upon the globe, in one time or another, have found there an asylum against invasion. At the same time as the uncultivated soil of the forests offers the enemy less fodder, it arrests the progress of a large calvary force—so threatening to an agricultural people. It is for this reason that the Moors left not a single bush in the two Castiles, which are still today almost entirely stripped of wood, and employ no combustible other than straw. The forests and the mountains are the fortresses of nature that protect the peoples who retire to them much more surely than our stone fortresses protect the armies shut up inside them.

Nor do I fear to say that the worst evil that can be inflicted upon a great people is to deprive them of forests. Deforestation was a badge of infamy that our feudal institutions meted out to noble felons; we ought not to inflict it upon ourselves. The greatest benefit which may be hoped for from a provident administration is the conservation, the management, and even the extension of the forests. It is deplorable that the only public good to have escaped the scythe of time, the hatchet of the Revolution, and the ravages of war, and which has been conserved and even added to by the usurper, might perish under the legitimate King, and that the Restoration would in this regard not only guarantee but complete the work of the Revolution. |•

NOTES

[1] "Opinion sur la Proposition de M. le comte de Blangy, et sur le Rapport de M. Roux de Laborie, relatifs à l'amélioration du sort du Clergé," February 7, 1816.

[2] "Opinion sur le Projet de loi relatif aux Elections," February 24, 1816.

[3] "Opinion sur le Budget de 1816," March 19, 1816.

[4] "Opinion sur les Elections," December 30, 1816, *Oeuvres,* VI: 329–33.

[5] "Opinion sur l'Article premier du Titre XI du projet de loi de Finances," March 4, 1817.

[6] Ibid.

7 | 1820
On Political Economy

AUGUSTE DE SAINT-CHAMANS has just published his reflections upon taxation and systems of political economy.[1] These reflections honor the quality of his mind, the breadth of his knowledge, and the independence of his judgment, and they bring to mind his published views on the electoral law.

Saint-Chamans's opinion on the electoral law—the most remarkable of all those published at the time—has since been vindicated by events. We cannot refrain from hoping for the same success for his latest work, in which he opposes the various systems of political economy of Adam Smith and his disciples, systems that will prove to be as disastrous as the electoral law was shown to be by the most recent elections.

Systems of political economy seem to have something in common with poetics.

Homer, consulting the great book of nature—the only one he seems to have had before him in those far-off days—made a poem that will forever be the model epic. Industrious writers have studied Homer and have attempted to trace from his model the rules of the art that he was the first to cultivate and to perfect. These rules are unnecessary to a man of genius and unprofitable to all others, for rules, in the imaginative arts, are useful only to those who, like Homer, could have invented them or rather discovered them. Bacon, indeed, could have described these rules—and spoken more truly than he did about *final causes*—as barren virgins.

In all times and places, nature has taught men to work and to exchange among themselves the fruits of their labor or industry. That is to say that she has taught them to live by devoting themselves to every kind of work necessary to the condition of their society. Some have had more success than others in this or that kind of work, and have executed it with greater perfection and ease: thence the division of labor and the diversification of trades.

As men spread about the earth, their labors multiplied with them, their produce with their labors, and their exchanges with their needs. As these exchanges became more varied and frequent, they everywhere gave birth to conventional signs as means of exchange that could represent every good and every value. In one place, metals, unformed or as coins, have fulfilled the office of these signs; in another, pearls, shells, or even simple denominations of abstract values.

At length, when the transport of these material signs had itself become expensive and difficult, men thought to write the signs themselves and send them in treaties or letters of exchange, and this gave rise to the various operations of banks and to all the speculations of commerce. None of these things was done or commanded by governments. Governments, finding all of them established, had only to protect them, and sometimes they have disturbed them by wishing to regulate them in ways other than the nature of things had done.

Men who were neither laborers, nor merchants, nor artisans, but who were writers working by their wits, made note of all these developments and wished to give learned explanations of these processes, or one might say of nature's art, and to teach how these things that everywhere came about by themselves were done or should have been done. They have made a science called political economy, which makes its student neither more economical nor more political, and with which, when one has read all the works to which it has given birth, one knows no better how to govern men than one who has read treatises of poetics knows how to write poems. This science is even considered to be useless by its professors, for according to them it leads only to this result: *Laissez-faire, laissez-passez.* And this can be done without either studies or books.

This laborious research, however, has led governments astray more than one might suspect by persuading those who ran them that they knew something about the great art of governing after studying the varied and frequently contradictory systems of political economy. By throwing governments exclusively into the material aspect of society—which fortunately takes care of itself more or less on its own, like eating and drinking, and is the family's concern rather than the State's—these systems have distracted them from the morals of society, which do not take care of themselves. In the moral life, men endlessly encounter passions that blind them to their duties, and they cannot do without the continual activity of governments. The administration of things has, therefore, lost sight of the direction of men, and when, from a desire to regulate all things, and to regulate them from a unique center and in a uniform manner, governments have been drowned in details, and have realized that the more arrangement there is of things, the less order and discipline there is among men. Preoccupied with political economy, governments have believed that there were not enough farmers, although everything was cultivated, including lands that ought not to have been; that there was not enough trade, although there was perhaps too much; not enough taxes, although everything was taxed, even doors and windows; not enough population, although even the smallest States had more men than they could rule; and not enough money, as if there could ever be enough to satisfy our thirst for it. At the same time they allowed themselves to be persuaded that there was too much religion, too much morality, too much severity in the laws, too much obedience in the State, too much dependence in the family, too much respect in the inferior classes toward the superior classes, not enough liberty, and not enough equality. Such great disorders could only come from a defect in the administration; and there were so many administrations and administrators! It must, they said, have come from a defect in the constitution. The sick were lacking a regime and a good temperament, so they set out to give temperaments to the sick, that is, constitutions. Sometimes the kings granted them, sometimes the people imposed them, and thanks to these constitutions—whether granted or imposed—Europe found itself in a moral and political disorder the likes of which has not been seen since the beginning of the world, a disorder against which the whole political economy of Adam Smith and the others is certainly powerless.

It has been said that we are beholding a vast drama, in which civilization, like a lovely princess, is in the clutches of base villains, and is saved from the uttermost evils only by luck or miracles. Neither the marvelous occurrences nor the requisite characters have we lacked. There are ferocious tyrants, timid bystanders, fools aplenty, scenes of carnage and fury, and a thousand catastrophes, but no happy ending. We still await the obligatory outcome of all such dramas: the punishment of the crime and the triumph of virtue.

This digression has taken me far afield from the work of Saint-Chamans. He argues successfully, it seems to me, against Adam Smith and his disciples, but not against Malthus, the author of the *Essay on the Principle of Population*. I must admit that I regretted to see Saint-Chamans rely upon the ridiculous argument of one of our modern writers of political economy, who, in order to refute the assertion of the famous Cambridge professor that the population grows to meet the means of subsistence, claims that one of our ancient noble families should now be so numerous as to be able to populate all of France by itself. He failed to see that the general truth does not apply to the particular, and that the trends in population of a State cannot be applied to the population of a family, which has its chances of premature death, widowhood, sterility, celibacy, and injuries, especially in those classes devoted to the profession of arms. Moreover, while no one in a wealthy family dies of hunger even when the general population is declining for want of subsistence, nevertheless the difficulty of living puts a stop to marriages and makes the survival of children more rare and their abandonment more common. This is the entire claim of Mr. Malthus, whose work is, in the science of administration, and in the administration not of things but of men, the most useful work to have appeared for a long time.

Yet there are in the work of Saint-Chamans two points of which one could have wished for a fuller treatment, considering the role that they play in every system of political economy; here I refer to luxuries themselves and to another very common luxury today, that of machines that multiply the products of industry while economizing on the labor of men. An author now already dated, Melon, has written in favor of luxury; a modern economist cited by Saint-Chamans has condemned it. It was a simple matter for Saint-Chamans to prove that this condemnation was inconsistent with his own system of political economy, and he himself sides with Melon. Luxury is not easy to define. One can hardly give an idea of it except by examples, and, in general, as it is always growing, the luxury of one time would have been simplicity and modesty at another.

One may say, in general, that any expenditure that exceeds a man's condition or the purpose of the object in question is a luxury. It would, for instance, be luxurious should a private individual–be he as rich as a king–wish to be lodged and waited upon as a sovereign. Given the purpose of the building, there is also luxury, I believe, in the construction of the stock exchange that is being built in Paris, the exterior of which will be more ornate than the loveliest church in the capital and than the palace of our kings.

Luxury springs from a noble principle in our nature: our restless quest for perfection. We have the good, we want the best, and we discover the useless and the superfluous. It is in the arts and not in moral things that the best is often the enemy of the good. Luxury, considered morally, softens the man, and makes him greedy, egotistical, and dependent upon a thousand artificial needs. In politics, and considered in the private individual, luxury causes the inevitable inequality of conditions and fortunes to be all too sensible. Where liberty and equality are made vague principles that each applies according to his own lights and passions, the luxury of the few standing in too strong a contrast with the poverty of the many makes the latter envious of the riches that provide so many pleasures.

In finance—and it is in this regard that our economists consider it—luxury multiplies work, favors the circulation of money, and allows the laboring classes to live. Nothing is more true, but one must not lose sight of the fact that it began by giving birth to them, and that a new industry introduced in a country ruins every old industry of the same kind that existed there, and will have soon raised up a new population that will always be on the brink of dying of hunger if the kind of industry to which it owes its existence comes to an end, either because of political events or by the caprice of fashion that turns toward a new and more fortunate industry. If there are today in France a million men employed in factories working upon cotton that comes to us from India, then this is as if we had brought a nation of Indians into France at the same time as we lifted the prohibition of working with cotton or even of selling Indians. I know that this effect might be a long time in being felt in a large country, but the moment when its results are manifest will be reached sooner for one people and later for another. It happened long ago in England, where, according to recent writings, there are six hundred thousand men of the industrial population who lack work and consequently the means of existence, and, falling to the care of the State, cause great trouble and continual worry. This dangerous effect has made itself manifest from time to time in parts of France, and as everywhere, thanks to industry, the working classes tend to gain in number of individuals while the superior classes, occupied with public service, remain stable or even shrink, and the proportion between the ignorant part of the nation and the enlightened, between those who know how to rule by the influence of their minds and by the ascendency of respect and consideration they enjoy, and those who must be ruled, that is to say the proportion between the physical force of society and its moral force, is completely unbalanced to the prejudice of the latter. Thence inevitably follow revolutions, which, since their timing is unknown to governments, must be the object of their constant surveillance and continual precaution.

In the past, the luxury of governments and even of wealthy individuals consisted in founding public institutions of religion, charity, public education, and the like. These did not cause the population to grow; instead they served to assist it and to aid the existing population in all its weaknesses of age, sex, and condition. Today wealth takes another direction, and is devoted principally to objects of purely material utility, to those establishments of industry and commerce that give birth to a new population for which they must subsequently provide a living. If you open a canal in order to transport more easily and cheaply those goods necessary to the provisioning of a large city, be assured that you will make it still larger by providing new ways of living there—and even living more agreeably if at the same time you multiply places to serve public pleasures—and you will make your cities more difficult to govern than whole kingdoms, and the capitals of States will become the capitals of revolutions.

To all of the kinds of luxuries introduced into Europe by the Revolution (for political disorders bring moral and economic ones in their train), has been added, first in England then later on the continent, the luxury of machines used to multiply the products of industry while economizing on the labor of men. It is curious that industry, which causes the population to grow beyond measure, has imagined a way of dispensing with men. Yet I do not know whether the establishment of these machines can be justified even in the eyes of liberty and equality, those two divinities of modern times. Nature, in condemning man to work, charged society with furnishing it to him, or at least leaving him at liberty to find it himself. Thus in every society there is a sum of agrarian or industrial labor necessary for the subsistence of that society and to all that this subsistence consists in. On pain of abject poverty, there must be sufficient production for its consumption and sufficient consumption for its production. The factory owner who creates a machine that allows ten or fifteen men (and frequently women and children) to do the work that would have taken him a hundred men or more to do before disturbs this natural proportion. The number of producers has decreased, but the production has increased. The consumers have remained, but their consumption has diminished, for the machines take away from a great many men the means of existence and consumption. There is, therefore, more production than consumption; and this is even now one of the causes of the stagnation of internal trade, for which commerce has no one to blame but itself. To reestablish the equilibrium, there must be machines of consumption set up beside these machines of production. Yet men alone can consume what the machines produce. It might be said that the men left at leisure by the creation of these machines will devote themselves to another kind of industry or to the creation of a new industry. Saint-Chamans notes with good reason that for a great many men this kind of change of occupation is almost impossible, and that today all the arts have made such great progress there are hardly any more new types of industry to hope for. Now, shall we believe that some men should be allowed in this way to disturb the order established by nature herself, both the proportion of producers to consumers and of production to consumption, on which so many needs and relations of so many different kinds repose? I do not believe it: Even the most unlimited liberty consists only in doing what does not injure another. This injustice, if it is one, is perceived by the people, and we may even note that it is too violently sensed by our neighbors, where the first acts of violence, in moments of disorder, are directed against these machines and their owners. Montesquieu, for this reason, voiced his doubts about the utility of the invention of mills for wheat, and, nevertheless, for this good of the first and absolute necessity, for every day and for everyone, there is no proportion between the producers and the consumers, inasmuch as one must nourish women, children, the elderly and infirm, strangers, prisoners, and so on. The work of men and animals was slow and imperfect, did not supply as much flour as wind or water mills, and did not, I believe, suffice for daily consumption. This is a case in which the machine has come to the aid of man.

I am aware that it is said that the legitimate reason for establishing these machines is the necessity of holding our own in the market against the competition from our neighboring nations who have introduced them in their own lands. Yet at the same time we would have foreign consumption account for the surplus of our production. By now our statesmen should be comparatively unmoved by such arguments, which grow weaker daily, as each nation establishes factories on its own soil and every government arms its borders with customs offices and defends itself against foreign products as against an invasion. The true politician is suspicious of the claim to have spun so fine a thread that the neighboring lands will all wish to buy it. He is, instead, far more likely to be concerned about the disorders that arise in a State from the alternation of ease and misery to which the industrial population is exposed, which, making the objects of industry without being able to consume them, is no less obliged to consume the fruits of the soil without the ability to produce or even to purchase them, and which, finding itself without work and without bread, is a ready-made instrument for revolution.

The statesman notes that at the same time as the invention of machines tends to accumulate industrial capital in a small number of hands, other causes tend to disperse agricultural capital in a great number of hands, that an industry of large machines is replacing that of smaller ones, and that power looms are causing the spinning wheel to be abandoned, while in agriculture small machines are replacing the large, and the spade and hoe are taking the place of the plow and wagon. In this way the whole land is covered with large factories and small farms, which, barely sufficient to nourish the agricultural population, do not have enough surplus to nourish the industrial population. Lifting his regard higher and beyond the material, he further notes that industry shuts men up in cities and corrupts them, while agriculture, on the contrary, scatters them about the countryside and preserves them from corruption by isolation and by more regular and constant labor. Perhaps then he will admire as the most useful lesson of political economy that maxim of the great master of morals, a maxim as true and as applicable to the government of societies as to the conduct of the private man: "Seek ye first order and justice, and all the rest shall be added unto you."

It is in vain that we depart from the plans of nature and would, in our foolish wisdom, substitute our own for them. Nature will take back her rights and lead us back to her laws by the disorders that follow upon our infraction of them. The establishment of machines and the division of the soil should at length produce an effect diametrically opposed to the one hoped for by their fanatical partisans, who, making the people the sovereign, wish to render them numerous so that they will be stronger than the checks that the government might oppose to their caprice. The parcel of land that in the first generation furnishes subsistence to a family, when divided and subdivided among the children, will by the third generation no longer nourish any of them. These infinitely small fractions of land, sold or abandoned, will enlarge the patrimony of some other family, who, sooner or later, will suffer the same fate. Then they will see that in an agricultural country families cannot endure without the right of primogeniture and the inequality of inheritance. On the other hand, since the establishment of large machines, industry makes use of a smaller number of arms, and men lacking landed property and finding inadequate means of existence will less often marry. Thus the proportion will gradually be reestablished between the landowning population and the industrial population, and by a necessary consequence, between the physical force and the moral force of society. If, that is, our liberals, with their doctrines and their schemes, leave us any society at all. |•

NOTES

[1] *Du système d'impôt fondé sur les principes de l'économie politique* (Paris, 1820).

8 | 1829
On Pauperism

PAUPERISM AND the abandonment of children are two bloody sores eating away at France. She does not lack for other ones. Yet these two are constantly worsening, and the end of their course cannot be foreseen. Nor may we hope that they will be healed as long as we continue to attempt only to lessen their effects without seeking to know their causes and to cure them at the root.

The doctor who treats a festering sore is not content to prescribe exterior applications and dressings, but he also most strenuously prohibits anything that might heat or irritate the humors and by prescribing a moderate diet he seeks to lighten and to purify the patient's blood.

The measures undertaken by the government against these two social scourges honor its generosity. Yet provisional measures will bring only temporary comfort to the sick. More powerful ones are required to lessen the intensity of the evil.

At present we shall restrict our attention to pauperism.

We were not shocked, but we were filled with grave foreboding by the recent appeal to the Parisians that their charity might come to the aid of our beggars, who are ineffectually assisted by laws that leave their numbers undiminished.

Today the great scenes of the Revolution and the long wars that followed it are no longer present to our minds. A long period of peace and security have allowed industry to unfurl all its sails, while our farmers have seen their labors rewarded with harvests that have always been sufficient, and at times abundant. Today the equality of inheritance has divided landed property and multiplied agricultural families, whose property decreases with each generation and will in the end disappear. All of these causes of the growth of the population were momentarily suspended by the Revolution, but, since the Restoration they have acted with redoubled energy. This is especially true of the laboring and proletarian population, whose growth is always more rapid on account of its numbers, and is encouraged still more by the great labors that luxury and necessity demand of it.

Let us not deceive ourselves, it is not—as is often said—the high cost of living or the scarcity of work that produce the evil of which we speak. These two temporary causes only make the poor more numerous in some areas. It is, rather, the low cost of living and the abundance of work that are the source of the general scourge of begging, for the works of industry give birth to more men than they can nourish. This is very different from agriculture, which nourishes those to whom it gives birth.

The products of agriculture, however improved one might suppose them to be, are nevertheless limited by the extent and the fertility of the soil. The productions of industry are limitless, as is the multiplication of mankind. It is with good reason that Mr. Malthus, the celebrated professor at Cambridge, has said that the products of agriculture grow arithmetically—1, 2, 3, 4, 5—while mankind grows geometrically—2, 4, 8, 16, and so on.

It cannot, therefore, be affirmed that the produce of the earth will grow at the same rate as the number of men employed to cultivate it. Yet it may be affirmed, and with certainty, that the products of industry will thus grow, and especially where men are not content to work upon the produce of the native soil in order to serve the needs of their neighbors, but instead work with primary materials from the four corners of the globe in order to satisfy the needs of the whole world.

Allow me briefly to compare the farmer to the industrial worker.

The farmer may not live any longer than the industrial worker, but he preserves his strength longer, because he exerts himself in most difficult and healthy labors, in the open air and always during the daytime. He is more sober and more temperate than the industrial worker, and his diet is better regulated and more healthy. If he rests on Sunday, he works on Monday. Agriculture has tasks for all ages, and the old man comes to the end of his career ends it as he began it, watching the children and the animals around the house.

The intelligence of the farm hand is kept very active by the variation in his work, and by the conduct, the reflection, and the knowledge required of one who cultivates the soil and husbands animals, while that of the industrial laborer is occupied his whole life with turning a crank, making a shuttle move back and forth, or pushing a lever.

Nor do I speak of the difference between the character and the habits of the farmer and the character and habits of the industrial worker, the independence of the former, who asks everything from nature and expects from her only the success of his labors, and the dependence of the other, who expects everything from man, and asks for things only from him.

Thus Lord Feldkirk, after having spoken of the martial spirit, the generous habits, and the exalted and romantic character of the Scottish highlanders, complained of their wont to emigrate to America[1] since the changes that had came over their land after the battle of Culloden: "If there is some means of retaining these men in their homes, it can only be the introduction of some new branch of industry. If we were to succeed in this, these men would take on the way of life and the habits of factory workers. They might, as have others, furnish a few recruits, but they would no longer resemble their ancestors."

The industrial laborer, given to sedentary work, shut up indoors, and often required to work at night—in order by this extraordinary labor to supplement his meager salary—is ill much more often than is the farmer. Exhausted from his constant, monotonous uniform work and from lack of sleep, he makes of intemperance a necessity. If he rests on Sunday, he is drunk on Monday. The farm hand is only paid annually, while he is paid weekly, and thus he more easily wastes his money gambling or in bars. He almost never saves anything against old age, nor for his family—and factory workers are almost all married. The community of the two sexes in the workshops of industry disposes them to marriage, which, contracted too early, does not even save them from libertinism. And when age and infirmity have spent their strength, having nothing saved for themselves or for their children, neither one of them has any resource save in begging or hospitals.

Industry employs the youth, and perhaps even too much so in a land that has need of soldiers, and assuredly cannot pay them the wages that industry can pay. This is what has defeated voluntary recruitment and has brought us to conscription. Industry also abandons the elderly and the infirm. In bygone days the government would have found effective ways to assist them through the guilds—an institution known throughout Europe—which could have been obliged to create an endowment for their care, and which often in fact did just that.

Let us listen to what the *Edinburgh Review*—certainly not a suspect source—reports in 1828 about the continually growing misery of England, bent under the unbearable yoke of the poor law.

"The population grows beyond measure, and yet the supply of labor is never equal to the demand. Some parishes have an excess of thirty, forty, or fifty laborers for whom no work can be found. Soon the effects correspond to the causes: Able-bodied men surrender themselves to debauchery. The father neglects his children, and the children do not even think of providing for their fathers; the masters and their servants are endlessly quarreling. Criminals display an ever-growing boldness, and England, in spite of its prisons and punishments, is infested with tramps and thieves. The workers are more and more degraded. Their number already surpasses all need for them, and if the new poor tax is allowed to bring forth its fruit, it will cover the land with the most abject poverty and misery, and all the industrial classes of society will henceforth live by charity."

"The poor-tax, in 1748, 1749, and 1750, for each of these years, raised 730,155 pounds sterling. In 1817 and 1818, it had grown to the enormous sum of 9,320,440 pounds sterling," which is to say more than 242 million francs. Here is grave matter for the consideration of our industrial economists!

Industry is, therefore, an extremely active and continually acting cause of the growth of the population, and it is more active to the extent that the low price of necessities and the abundance of work hastens and favors this development. For when a spinning wheel is a dowry, a weaver a man of means, and a weaver's loom a sharecropper's farm, there will be more marriages and more children will be born. There are consequently more beings than industry can now employ, and others to come whom it will never be able to employ at all; there will be, therefore, more misery and more begging.

It is so plain that industry is the fertile mother of an indigent population that Malthus desired to force a great part of the working class to abstain from marriage, and Scarlett, another member of the Commons, and, I believe, a writer on economic topics, proposed a bill in the parliament of England that would work toward the same goal. It is surely a remarkable thing that Protestant writers, who have so often spoken against the voluntary celibacy of the Catholic religion, would recommend forced celibacy, although in fact, to save the appearances, they call it only a "moral constraint."

To be convinced of the immense progress made by industry (whose benefits are all that is ever spoken of), one need only glance at France and Europe. Thanks to industry, we see villages become towns, towns become cities, and the enlarging of prisons, hospitals, penal colonies, places where tramps are kept, all of these finding their place on this vast, seductive canvas.

One ought not believe that it is in the interest of humanity for a certain party to push with all its strength for the excessive development of industry and endlessly complain that the government does not sufficiently favor its progress, even when industry is at the heights of prosperity. This party holds in reserve for itself the immense workshop of the revolution, which it gives as an occupation to the whole industrial population—to all ages and to both sexes—for everyone is capable of destroying things, and if one were to give a band of children the chateau of the Tuileries to demolish, the smaller ones would break the windows, the bigger ones set fire to the structure, and all of them together would not build even a shepherd's hut.

Another extremely active cause of the growth of poverty is the ever-increasing division of landed property at each new generation, which has found an answer to the problem of the infinite divisibility of matter. In fact, if you suppose that a family always lives at ease with a landed property of a certain value, when the family is obliged to divide it among all its children—who, once landowners, will all want to have a family—at the first division this property will be reduced almost in half. At the second and third divisions, the property of each one will be further and further reduced until it is infinitesimally small. At last, when the man who possesses a strip of property has worn out himself and the soil in trying to eke an existence from it, he dies young and leaves his family in misery.

It should also be noted that today industry employs large machines and agriculture little ones. We spin with machines that have the strength of a hundred or two hundred horses, and we cultivate with the spade and the hoe. While there are some large landowners who cultivate with powerful tools, like the rich farmer who today uses the techniques of the farm of Rouville and the Belgian plow, they can see into the future to the time when their children will be forced to dig with a spade, and, as one large landowner said to this author, will perhaps one day be farmhands where today they are masters.

Doubtless this farming by hand can produce a little bit more wheat or potatoes on the same piece of land in a given time. But can a great landowning nation be satisfied with the kind of farming that never produces a surplus or a reserve, and, having nourished a large population at great pains, can, at the first gusts of ill weather, leave it entirely vulnerable to the pain and the degradation of famine?

In the past, religion was charged with feeding the poor, and it generously acquitted itself of this pious duty: No town lacked its convents, no countryside was without some wealthy monastery nearby. The poor went from one to another, and did not, as today, all gather in the same places. These large properties were well-cultivated and well-built. They were farmed by men who were not driven by greedy masters and who looked to the future with tranquility. They therefore often made great fortunes. These large properties were veritable granaries of abundance, the only kind that can be established and kept secure. If one were to complain that their abundant alms encouraged idleness, then at least it might be said that in making the poor, religion fed them, while industry makes them but does not feed them.

Those who acquired the wealth of the clergy did not inherit these charges, and the government is today the only and the greatest distributor of public assistance. Yet the poor man receives alms from the hands of religion as a benefit; he receives it from the hands of the government as a debt, because he knows that the government can require as a tax what he today receives as a free gift, and that, if it at its own expense nourishes, lodges, dresses, and keeps in its houses of detention and correction those troops of miscreants and vagabonds, it must give bread to men who are only poor.

This solemn appeal to public beneficence, if undertaken once and, I hope, with success, will be repeated as many times as necessary. And, as the number of poor should, as we have proved, grow with the progress of industry, and just as much with its successes as with its reverses, and also grow with the continual repetition of the equality of inheritance, the continuity of needs should lead, sooner or later, to the continuity of measures taken to care for them. What is this new continuity of beneficence if not a new poor tax? Is not the forced upkeep of hospitals and houses of correction and detention already a poor tax?

In France, we will have recourse to a poor tax sooner than the English, who, after the rape of their monastic establishments, found themselves in a situation much like the one in which we find ourselves today. To prevent pauperism, which soon after became an appalling problem, the English took measures that humanity and the Catholic religion would not allow even against criminals.

Let us allow the historians to speak.

We find the beginning of the poor laws in an act of the twenty-seventh year of the reign of Henry VIII. This act authorized the sheriffs, the magistrates, and the churchwardens to raise voluntary alms, and at the same time to punish beggars who persevered in their condition by cutting off part of their ear, and even by putting them to death as criminals if they returned to begging.

The young Edward began his reign with an act that punished beggars by having them marked with a hot iron and reduced to slavery for two years, and by giving their masters the right to make them wear an iron collar and to feed them on bread and water.

Elizabeth, having attempted in vain three times in succession to care for the poor with alms, made the obligatory act that is in force today called the poor tax, which has become a weighty charge upon landowners, as we have seen.

During this reign and the preceding ones, licenses to beg were given; but in the end they had to return to a compulsory tax.

After the reign of William—and when the English had created a bank and public debt—the number of the poor grew so out of proportion that the parliament appointed a commission to study the matter and to propose a remedy.

Locke was a member of this commission, and he said in his report that the multiplication of poor and the necessity of raising the tax to care for them was so well attested to throughout the world that he could not have a single doubt about the subject, and that, if one wanted to inquire into the causes of this, one would find them *not in the scarcity of necessities or in the lack of work*, but in the slackening of discipline and the corruption of morals.

Under the reign of Anne, Defoe, another writer on economic subjects, thought that no help should be given to the poor, and he attributed their poverty to their crimes and their excesses, without himself—or Locke—ever asking what was the origin of a corruption of morals that had been unknown in England before the Reformation.

There is far too much reasonableness and humanity in France for us to be carried to such extreme measures against beggars, and this is what makes me say that after having used up the means of persuasion and voluntary gifts to care for the poor, if we are ever forced to come to obligatory measures, we will turn to them much sooner than the English did.

Yet England, with a population only half of ours, finds in its vast colonies and in a commerce that embraces the whole globe, in its large and indivisible properties, and the nomadic temperament of its inhabitants, and the great demand for men that its shipping creates—England, I say, finds means to employ and to feed the poor part of the nation that do not exist to the same degree in France.

The extension and the multiplicity of industrial enterprises that create immense fortunes in capital to the profit of democracy, the ever-growing division of landed property, which ruins and destroys large fortunes in landed property to the detriment of the monarchy, are two plain and incontestable scourges. As if it were not enough to divide landed property, private speculators take the greater part of sales made in small lots while bands of buyers travel over France purchasing large properties in order to sell them again in smaller lots. This is a kind of commerce in which the speculators doubtless find great profits, but which seems to have been inspired as a kind of appendix to the Revolution and the kind of redistribution of land that has been the dream of all democratic states.

It seems, however, that industry digs its own grave when we see all the governments, possessed with the same fury for industry—always wanting to sell while at the same time wanting to buy as little as possible—favor exports, restrict imports, surround themselves with an army of toll collectors to push back from their borders the products of foreign industry, and today, when machines have made processes the same everywhere, seek to create a purely national industry.

The machines that mechanical science daily creates or perfects have not been in use for long enough for one to judge with certitude the effect that they will produce upon society. Yet if one may be permitted a conjecture, we may believe that the immense quantity of manual labor that they save—while multiplying production to infinity—should by diminishing work also diminish the population, and consequently consumption. Is this not already the cause to which must be attributed the low prices of certain industrial products that were sold at a much higher price when a larger number of better paid men was required to produce them?

There seems to be a certain contradiction inherent in using machines to produce while demanding many men to consume and at the same time reducing to the lowest level possible the wages of those few whom the machines employ. Thus we have seen, particularly in England, whole populations of workers act out their rage against the machines themselves and at the same time demand higher wages.

It is remarkable that while we complain of the multitude and the importunity of the poor, our legislative assemblies attend only to fiscal savings and reductions in salaries. We must, however, be on our guard in establishing an immense workshop of industrial labor in a continental and almost exclusively agrarian nation, lest consumption fail to equal production, and production be forced to stop or to reduce the number or the wages of the workers. It is the office of the land to support industry. Now, the government is in some sense the channel by which landed property comes to the aid of industry. It fulfills this duty or necessity in two ways, either by taxing property directly in order to care for the indigent, as it has done in England with the poor tax, or in giving its agents at all levels of the administration salaries that are, on the one hand, the legitimate reward for their services and the just compensation for their having renounced lucrative occupations in order to take up public service, and, on the other, the means of their living honorably and decently and making the government honorable in its agents. I am not at all one who would augment administrative salaries; I should even like, if I thought it possible, to suppress the taxes that are raised by constraint, such as the tax on land, which is almost entirely suppressed in England. I would have the citizen pay only voluntary taxes, such as are indirect taxes. I even hold that in a *frank* nation, as was that of the Franks, our ancestors, except for extraordinary dangers to the State that call for extraordinary measures, there should not be compulsory service except for the wicked, and that the man—the family man, the domestic man—should not be employed in public service except by his own choice. So far as I can see, it is in this and this alone that public liberty consists.

Thus, in a great landowning nation in which industry has taken such a sudden rise, and in which it has formed an immense population that can only live by industrial labor, it is only with a religious circumspection that we should throw ourselves into a system of reductions and economies. Even luxury—of which I am no partisan—serves industry, and when we have let things progress to their current state in France, it is only by incremental measures that one can destroy or stop the course of the river that fertilizes so vast a land. A reduction of the land tax, hardly noticeable upon property as much divided as is that of France, or of indirect taxation, still less noticeable over our immense consumption, may, however, be infinitely prejudicial to industry and work against the measures the government has taken to satisfy its needs. One must even consider that what is done by public beneficence falls ultimately to the charge of private charity, and that is once again a new tax.

Yet what are all the efforts of private charity or public beneficence in the face of such pressing needs? What are even 200,000 francs, the sum the journals tell us has already been raised by the proposed subscription?

Seize, therefore, every means by which foreign trade may be made to prosper in a land, cover it with workshops and factories, render the circulation of money more rapid, and at all costs force the population to grow beyond what religion can instruct, what the government can contain, and sometimes even beyond what agriculture or commerce can nourish: then you may hold it for certain that you will need to shut up one part of this artificial population in prisons, poor houses, and hospitals, and subject the other part to rationing. Thus the natural order is overturned. Man should find his subsistence in the family that gives birth to him, and when he seeks it from the State—which neither *labors nor spins*—the government can only give him one by taking away from others, nourish the indigent families at the expense of landowning families, nor aid the poor without making others ill at ease. Private charity then becomes a subsidy, and public beneficence oppression. When there was neither commerce nor money in European society, the generous dreamt of putting a chicken in every pot. Today when nations vomit forth money, and cover the seas with their shipping and the markets with their goods, philosophy throws him into the economic soup.

Let it not be thought, after all that I have said about industry, that I am its detractor or its enemy. I am the enemy of nothing that contributes to the ornamentation and the well-being of society. On the contrary, I honor a wise industry, and rise up only against its indiscreet and excessive growth, which too often finds in itself the cause of own ruin; and, in this, I have on my side the testimony of able men in England who, on the subject of industry and its influence upon society, are judges against whom there is no appeal. |•

NOTE

[1] It is this emigration to America, after all of the changes caused by industry, that is the subject of one of the most perfect of English poems, *The Deserted Village* by Goldsmith, extracts from which Abbé Delille has so felicitously translated in his *Homme des Champs*.

9 | 1829
On Foundling Children

THE CONVENTION, hideous to remember, granted payments to unwed mothers, and the author of this essay much later saw some of them, babe in arms, come to the door of the Ministry of Interior, to claim the reward promised to their shameful fertility. Surely the like has never been seen in the laws of any nation. Perhaps the illegitimate births were intended to replace the many unjust deaths ordered by our legislative executioners, and debauchery thus made to compensate for murder.

Children, once born, must be provided for, and so poor houses were required to place a hatchway in their doors that need only be opened and shut in order to abandon a child to the care of the State.

And so at one time the laws encouraged illegitimate births, while at another, they facilitated the abandonment of children.

The intention of this last measure was to prevent infanticide. Yet if one were to consult the registers of our judges, he would be convinced that it has never been more frequent than in our day, and, unfortunately, that the infanticides that we learn of only point to the many more that are kept secret.

The infant is sacred only in the eyes of religion. In the eyes of politics, which cannot make use of its weakness, it is useless and without value. Thus the public exposure of infants was practiced among idolatrous peoples, such as the Chinese, who sacrifice them by the hundreds to the spirit of the river, as Lord Marcartney said. It was practiced by even the most strictly ruled of ancient peoples, the lone exception being the Jews, who marked their children with the seal of religion by circumcision, as do the Muslims, who took the custom from them. It is well-known that among the Romans, the newborn child was placed at the feet of the father who allowed it to live only by raising it from the earth, thence our expression "to raise a child."

Religion alone protects the weakness of age as well as that of sex or of condition. We are unaware of how many infants—even illegitimate ones— have been saved by the necessity of baptism when the people were more religious, and still less can we count those still saved by the Church's public prohibition–on the pain of excommunication–of mothers and nurse-maids to place their children in bed with them before a certain age, that they might not risk suffocating them while they sleep.

The measures of which we have just spoken that encourage illegitimate unions have borne their fruit.

One need only consult the registry of poor houses in order to be convinced of the prodigious increase in the number of foundling children. In the statistics of the city of Paris, we have seen their number rise to above one-third of the total number of births, and I have myself verified that the poor houses of smaller towns, which never in the past had more than eighteen or twenty to feed, now have almost three hundred.

It may be believed that the number has risen in every *département*—Paris excepted—in a way approximately proportionate to their respective populations, and that if one were to count a greater number in some less populous and poorer *départements*, this is doubtless because in these *départements* religion has more force—less, perhaps, to prevent weakness than to prevent the crimes that attack the life of the infant before or after his birth.

The government has been alerted to the excessive multiplication of foundling children by its budget and has been obliged to support them with all that they have ready at hand for the needs of the *départements*. Many of these, in turn, have in their despair demanded a return to the law of Henri II that enforced declarations of expectancy. The government has undertaken two measures, not in order to decrease the growth of this miserable population—for that is beyond its power—but to care for its finances, for the poor houses, and for the *départements*.

It has, therefore, been decreed that children placed with wet-nurses be given a collar or thin cord of silk, with the ends joined together under a leaden seal, and that children below the ages of ten to twelve years be transferred from one *département* to another. Inspectors have traveled across the *départements* in order to enforce the execution of these measures, and have paid the poor houses for the cost of the necessary collars and seals.

To me it seems that these two measures demonstrate their designer's good intentions more than his knowledge of the customs, prejudices, sentiments, and habits of the people, for the majority of those whose trade is to busy themselves with the people have rarely seen them except through their windows.

In the adopting these measures, the government has been guided by two ideas that come more from a spirit of philanthropy than from the truth.

It was believed that the poor houses sheltered a great many legitimate children, secretly abandoned by their parents. It is so easy and so secretive to abandon a child by passing him through the hatchway in the poor house door that one cannot know whether the children so abandoned are legitimate. All the same, if it were the case, it is because it is so easy for those who wish to be rid of their own child to abandon it.

The government is therefore persuaded that the tenderness of the parents will be awakened when they see their legitimate children ready to be marked on the collar with the indelible seal of bastardy (which is itself an evil) or to be transported far from their families into a foreign *département*. Yet as the parents could have been forced to abandon their children only by an extreme poverty that almost always leaves them bereft of the means to reclaim them one day, what will these miserable children gain by it except to die of hunger and cold in a family that might not be their own, or to go from door to door begging their poor sustenance, instead of being nourished, clothed, and lodged in a poor house? If, on the other hand, one were to suppose that the parents had possessed the means to nourish them but had exposed them from avarice, then it follows that they would be abandoned to public infamy should their crime be revealed. Certain of never being discovered, unnatural parents such as these would surely prefer to leave them in the poor house to which they had already been abandoned.

The other idea that has seduced and misled the government is that the wretches who have given birth to these illegitimate children would take them back home rather than see them marked with the fatal collar and separated from them and their country.

Yet the high-minded sentiments of unwed mothers for their children are generally seen only in novels, in which the mothers ordinarily finish by marrying their seducer. These wretches are almost always poor country girls, servants who have been seduced by their master or by the butler. Sent away from the master's house and banished from their parents' home for their bad conduct, having neither hearth nor home: What would we have her do with a child she is obliged to nourish, whose needs or whose very presence is enough to prevent her from earning a living, gaining employment, or finding a husband? The majority of them, almost all of them, would be most grateful to be rid of their children and to speak no more of them. It would be a great scandal in the towns, where moral license is all too common, and a still greater one in the countryside, where good morals are better preserved, to see the spectacle of these miserable girls carrying the fruits of their weakness. It would end all too often by their undertaking the prostitute's trade in order to survive, and thus carrying disorder and division into the bosom of families and marriages.

Perhaps the novelty of these unexpected measures has, in their initial moments, removed a few children from the poor houses. The inspectors will doubtless trumpet their success. Yet it is the wet-nurses who have shown a truly maternal tenderness for these poor children. Only with tears have they put the collar on children whom they could not keep at their own homes, and only with extreme regret have they seen many of them separated from their country, without hope of ever seeing it again. These miserable little beings are loved only by the good Sisters who direct the poor houses and by their wet-nurses. Some children, guarded by foster fathers after they have been weaned, have even remained in their adoptive homes, and sometimes have even married the children of the home. This would seem to be the door on which we ought to knock, if we wish better to provide for the moral and physical well-being of these children.

I can, moreover, hardly consider the ordinance that would remove foundling children from their *département* as a measure that will threaten the parents who abandoned them, nor can I conceive of its mode of execution. If it could be carried out, then these children, transplanted into places where they will be neither known nor loved by anyone, where no one will claim them or take any interest in them, will be greeted with the disdain and indifference that one shows for strangers marked with the seal of bastardy, and will be only an expense for the land that receives them. These children will only be more likely to end up homeless vagabonds prey to all the disorders of that condition.

These measures, I repeat, might momentarily lighten the burden that weighs upon the State, the poor houses, and the *départements*, but they will also compromise the physical and moral existence of these unfortunate beings.

The large population of foundling children is therefore a great scourge, and it is, moreover, an incurable scourge in the present state of our society, and, like that of pauperism, it will only increase.

In the past, abandoned children were nourished at the expense of the lords of the land in which they were found, whether the manor belonged to the king or to other lords, and the royal administrators, in the royal domain, and the manorial administrators, in the others, took great care to require pregnant girls, in accord with the law of the Henri II, to make declarations of expectancy that would place the life of the unborn child under the protection of the law; more importance was attached to this than to the honor of the mother, which was already compromised. I know of lands where the former lords would have refused to take back all of the honors and revenues they had lost through the laws of the Revolution, if they could not have taken them back except at the expense of nourishing abandoned children.

The severe measure of the declarations of expectancy contributed effectively to diminish the number of illegitimate births and prevented infanticide. Several *départements* have requested that we return to it, and if the measures undertaken by the government have no success, every *département* will soon demand it. It is, I believe, one of the desires of the departmental councils that has most won them the anger of the liberals, naturally opposed as they are to everything favorable to order and the well-being of society.

The government, which has inherited all of the manorial jurisdictions of the kingdom, is therefore today charged with the support of all the abandoned children, and the portion of the upkeep that it leaves to the charge of the poor houses and the *départements* falls in the last analysis upon the public.

I have seen the time when the weakness of a village woman produced in the countryside almost the same consternation as a murder, and was just as rare. In those days our morals were better because there was more respect for religion. For good morals are made by religion, and not by the police or the national guard.

If, however, something might shock us today, it is that there still remains some religious sentiment, even after all that has been done to rip it out of the hearts of the people, after the examples of impiety and immorality given by the Revolution, and the license of morals and libertinism of mind that the youth picked up in the military camps, and especially after the contagion of irreligious doctrines and by the disorder spread by design even to our thatched huts by the incredible profusion of corrupting writings given away or sold at a low price.

Virtuous instructors once made successful efforts to stop the withering contagion of impiety, but they were taken away from us, and in their wake have echoed the complaints of fathers of families.

The liberals were in competition with the Jesuits for the education of the youth, and they have, for that reason, demanded the suppression of their colleges. By ceding to this request, the government has done injury to respectable families and scandalized the Catholics. It has chosen for purely political motives to give way to a desire that was entirely irreligious. Now, in every establishment of public or private education, religion is but a course like Greek or mathematics. A college staffed by religious is, on the contrary, like a parish. Children can be taught about religion in a class, but they can be moved by it only in Church, and to children, as even to highly educated men, religion is more a matter of sentiment than of knowledge.

I have been shocked to read in a newspaper belonging to the ministerial party an article calling the Jesuits "devout Omars who have declared war upon the human mind." Have they, like Omar, burned libraries and declared war upon the human mind, those religious who educated all our great men, and all our great poets, even Voltaire and Delille? This is not even to speak of their own literary works. Have they, like Omar, made conquests with the sword, those peaceful legislators of Paraguay, who founded there, with the Cross and at the price of their blood, that beautiful civilization so justly admired by Montesquieu and so many others? The

Jesuits so many Omars! Let us read what the author of the *Genius of Christianity* said of them when he wrote in defense of religion and of the institutions that it has produced: "The Jesuits knew science and the world. The Benedictines were wise men, the Jesuits men of letters. Since their fall, education has not been raised up as high again. One cannot but mourn the loss of these teaching orders, uniquely occupied with literary researches and the education of youth. After a revolution that has weakened the bonds of morals and interrupted the course of studies, a pious and prudent society would seek a remedy for the cause of our woes. It is high time that we be alarmed by the condition in which we have been living for several years. Let us consider the generation we are now raising in our towns and in our countryside, those children who, born during the Revolution, have never heard of God, of the immortality of their soul, or of the punishments or rewards that await them in the next life. Let us consider what might become of such a generation, if we do not hasten to apply the remedy to the wound."

Our era is afflicted by our penchant to be always writing without having read anything. This same journal, while grossly libeling the Jesuits, has only honeyed words or, at most, tender reproaches for the *Constitutionnel and the Courrier.** It is a kind of fixed idea with them, by which they imprudently come close to expressing what is said in the liberal press. In calling the Jesuits "devout Omars" they doubtlessly meant only that they did not like the liberty of the press. But the human mind, like water, may be lifted up only with great effort. Voltaire himself would have been greater, and his glory more lasting and pure, if he had only been a tragic poet, and if he had not been permitted those irreligious sarcasms that superficial minds prejudiced against religion took to be philosophy.

We are familiar enough with impiety in the elevated classes of society. Lacking religion, these people at least cherish the sentiments of polite society, mutual self-respect, and the appearances that must be kept up in public. We do not, however, sufficiently comprehend the disorders that irreligion produces among rude men, those incapable of reflection, who lack sentiments of respect, who attach no price to the weight of public esteem,

---

* EDITOR'S NOTE: The *Constitutionnel* and the *Courrier* were left-wing papers with an anti-clerical bent.

and who lend themselves to every fit of passion. The large number of offenses against chastity, which echo about our tribunals, is the proof of this. We especially fail to comprehend what license has been given to our minds and our morals—perhaps more slowly, but also more deeply—by the inconceivable disdain that the succeeding governments of forty years in France have displayed for the sanctity of marriage. They have banished from their legal order the requirement that a religious ceremony consecrate the conjugal bond, and they have confided a parody of it to the libertine leniency of the town official, or to the rude ignorance of the village mayor who unites the spouses in the name of the law with the same indifference that he signs a passport or a writ of citizenship. In times of barbarism, man made war on man; in times of civilization, or rather in the police state, he makes war on woman, by making war on the religion that took her weakness under its protection and assured her social existence by marking her union with her spouse with the seal of immutability, and thus raising an association of interests to the dignity of an indissoluble society.

The obstinate refusal to place the necessity of nuptial benediction in the civil law was a shameful concession to the weak and false doctrines that refused to this great act of human and social life, consecrated by religion, the dignity of the sacrament, and which would make the conjugal bond into a temporary lease, dissoluble at the will of the parties, and the marriage into an eventual polygamy. Yet the legal necessity of a nuptial benediction, which in no way opposes the liberty of worship—inasmuch as each may have his marriage blessed by his own minister—has been reestablished in all the States from which the French Revolution had banished it, and France today is the only Catholic State where this religious law, the first and the most important of political laws, is not in force. Fortunately, the good sense and the faith of the people have corrected the failings of the legislator, and there are few Catholic families—and hardly any among the higher classes—who do not have their marriages blessed. Even those who are most opposed to this necessary law, if they profess the Catholic religion, ask this blessing for their marriage and for those of their children, and would not refuse to have it under pain of dishonor.

Everything, therefore, seems ready for the reestablishment of this law, proposed in the Chamber of 1815 by Monsieur de la Cheze-Murel, deputy from the *département* of Lot, and the report of which—made by the author of this essay in the name of the commission, and since published—was not able to be submitted to the Chamber before the end of the session. A certain party sees in this lacuna in our legislation a foundation stone for the reestablishment of divorce, the only ground that the Revolution has lost, and the first that it would take back again if it is ever able to seize the reins of power.

The example of so many unions formed only by the civil law, when France ceased to be Catholic and Christian, has weakened the respect for marriage more than one might think. If it was not a means of gaining a fortune in certain instances, many young men would end by dispensing with the civil act, as they dispense with the religious act, and would thus taste the sweetness of marriage without having the bother and the expense of it. It is in this way that the illegitimate unions so common today are propagated, the too-numerous fruits of which have provoked the solicitude of the government. We know that at the end of the Roman republic, indifference for a religion, which, though pagan, also had its ceremonies for consecrating the conjugal union, and a disgust for the bonds of marriage had made so much progress that Augustus saw himself to be obligated to ordain it by law. And he was not obeyed.

The government is therefore wrong to complain of the prodigious growth of the fruits of illegitimate unions while neglecting to give to legitimate unions the only character that can make their sanctity respected and their duration assured. |•

| Index